Cambridge Elements

Elements in Global Philosophy of Religion
edited by
Yujin Nagasawa
University of Oklahoma

SEMI-SECULAR WORLDVIEWS AND THE BELIEF IN SOMETHING BEYOND

Carl-Johan Palmqvist
Lund University

Francis Jonbäck
The University of Gävle and Uppsala University

Shaftesbury Road, Cambridge CB2 8EA, United Kingdom

One Liberty Plaza, 20th Floor, New York, NY 10006, USA

477 Williamstown Road, Port Melbourne, VIC 3207, Australia

314–321, 3rd Floor, Plot 3, Splendor Forum, Jasola District Centre, New Delhi – 110025, India

103 Penang Road, #05–06/07, Visioncrest Commercial, Singapore 238467

Cambridge University Press is part of Cambridge University Press & Assessment, a department of the University of Cambridge.

We share the University's mission to contribute to society through the pursuit of education, learning and research at the highest international levels of excellence.

www.cambridge.org
Information on this title: www.cambridge.org/9781009452212

DOI: 10.1017/9781009452199

© Carl-Johan Palmqvist and Francis Jonbäck 2025

This publication is in copyright. Subject to statutory exception and to the provisions of relevant collective licensing agreements, no reproduction of any part may take place without the written permission of Cambridge University Press & Assessment.

When citing this work, please include a reference to the DOI 10.1017/9781009452199

First published 2025

A catalogue record for this publication is available from the British Library

ISBN 978-1-009-45221-2 Hardback
ISBN 978-1-009-45218-2 Paperback
ISSN 2976-5749 (online)
ISSN 2976-5730 (print)

Cambridge University Press & Assessment has no responsibility for the persistence or accuracy of URLs for external or third-party internet websites referred to in this publication and does not guarantee that any content on such websites is, or will remain, accurate or appropriate.

Semi-Secular Worldviews and the Belief in Something Beyond

Elements in Global Philosophy of Religion

DOI: 10.1017/9781009452199
First published online: March 2025

Carl-Johan Palmqvist
Lund University

Francis Jonbäck
The University of Gävle and Uppsala University

Author for correspondence: Francis Jonbäck, francis.jonback@hig.se

Abstract: An increasingly large part of the population in the West identifies as religious Nones. Contrary to what might be assumed, most of them are not outright atheists. They reject traditional religion, but many pursue different forms of spirituality, and many entertain supernatural ideas. This Element concerns the worldview of these 'semi-secular' Nones. When asked whether they believe in God, they usually provide answers like 'Perhaps not God per se, but I do believe in something'. Belief in 'something' is the ontological cornerstone of many Nones' worldviews. The authors reconstruct it as the view 'Somethingism'. They assess Somethingism by inquiring how well it stands up to the epistemic challenge of being true to the demands of reason. They also assess it by exploring how it manages the existential challenge of providing comfort and guidance in this life, and its ability to align us with any transcendent reality there might be.

Keywords: religious Nones, worldviews, spirituality, Somethingism, secularity

© Carl-Johan Palmqvist and Francis Jonbäck 2025

ISBNs: 9781009452212 (HB), 9781009452182 (PB), 9781009452199 (OC)
ISSNs: 2976-5749 (online), 2976-5730 (print)

Contents

1 Introducing the Worldview of the Nones 1

2 Towards a Philosophical Understanding of Somethingism 12

3 The Rationality of Somethingism 27

4 Living with Somethingism 42

5 Summary and Future Research on Somethingism 58

References 62

1 Introducing the Worldview of the Nones

In recent decades, the religious landscape of Western society has been transformed by the rise of the 'Nones'. Nearly 30 per cent of the population in the United States and Canada, and more than 50 per cent in Europe, particularly Scandinavia[1] and Eastern Europe, no longer identify with traditional, communal religion (Jenkins 2019; Lemos & Puga-Gonzalez 2021; Norris & Inglehart 2011; Pew Research Center 2013; Pew Research Center 2024; Wilkins-Laflamme 2014; Willander 2020). Surprisingly, many of these individuals do not align with atheism or secular worldviews. They do not fit the traditional religious mould, but neither are they fully secularised in the sense of eschewing every supernatural idea. Borrowing a term from Ann af Burén (2015), we prefer to think of them as 'semi-secular'.[2]

The semi-secular Nones display remarkable diversity. In this group we find (among other things) believers in vague higher powers or life-forces (Willander 2020: 64), eclectic spiritualists who combine bits and pieces from a multitude of religious and secular traditions into a homebrew worldview of their own (Burton 2020; Mercadante 2014: 173; Pew Research Center 2009), people who through yoga, reiki, or other new spiritual practices find a sort of inner-life spirituality or divine spark within themselves (Heelas and Woodhead 2005; Mercadante 2020), and individuals who, sometimes with inspiration from indigenous contexts, find existential meaning in connection with nature (Thurfjell 2020; Wilkins-Laflamme 2022).

While these new semi-secular views and ideas have been investigated by sociologists and religious scholars for at least two decades, they have yet to seriously catch the attention of philosophers of religion. The purpose of this Element is to introduce semi-secular worldviews as a topic for philosophical investigation. We achieve this by focusing on Somethingism, the abstract view without details that 'something' exists. In academic circles it is sometimes known under Ronald Plasterk's Dutch term 'Ietsism' (Holstein 2020). We consider Somethingism not primarily as an independent worldview, but as a foundational part in many of the worldviews embraced by semi-secular Nones. Before turning our eyes exclusively to Somethingism, we begin by introducing the worldview framework and by offering a broad survey of the

---

[1] Although not identifying or committing to the central doctrines of any traditional religion, in Scandinavia most Nones still belong to a traditional Protestant Christian church. They are what is often referred to as 'cultural Christians' (Demerath 2000).

[2] Other terms used by scholars to describe this or similar phenomena include 'fuzzy religion' (Voas 2009), 'religiously remixed' (Burton 2020), or 'non-binary worldviews' (Bråten 2022). Yet another alternative would be 'semi-religious', but we prefer semi-secular as it connects with the grand narrative of Western secularisation.

worldviews of the semi-secular Nones (which henceforth we are simply going to refer to as 'Nones', thereby leaving the fully secular subgroup outside the discussion unless otherwise stated).

1.1 Worldviews

A worldview, as we understand it, serves as a lens through which individuals perceive and interpret the world around them. It encompasses their values as well as fundamental commitments, assumptions, and beliefs about, for example, the nature of reality, human existence, and the meaning of life. While some scholars argue that worldviews are '*total* picture[s] of the world' (Plantinga 2011: ix) or '*overall* view[s] of the nature of reality' (Cottingham 2014: 1), we want to emphasise that a worldview need not be comprehensive. [Italics added for emphasis.]

However, some standard components are included in most worldviews, such as the following:

Ontological components:	A view about what exists and what reality ultimately consists of.
Cosmological components:	A view about the beginning of everything that exists, where it comes from and how it all ends.
Epistemological components:	A view about knowledge or rational belief and how one obtains it.
Axiological components:	A view about goods and evils and the meaning of life.
Praxeological components:	A view about how to obtain human goods and how to live a meaningful life.[3]

Worldview components sometimes intertwine. Traditional religious worldviews may, for example, include God as a fundamental ontological component, together with the idea that God provides human existence with purpose and meaning (praxeological components) as well as morality (axiological component) and an explanation of everything (cosmological component). In the fourth section of this Element, we will pay special attention to the way in which ontological components might be what we can call *existentially and morally significant*. More general questions which will run as a central theme throughout the Element are whether the worldviews of the Nones contain something which has a role akin to that of God in traditional religion, and if so, what can we say about this 'something'.[4]

---

[3] See also Stenmark (2022b: 571–572) and Taves (2020).
[4] A relevant question also elaborated by, for example, Taylor (2007: 9).

Semi-Secular Worldviews and the Belief in Something Beyond

Worldview theory provides an overarching framework which enables the analysis of the fundamental commitments and practices of religious individuals, as well as the commitments and practices of those who identify themselves as Nones, be they semi-secular or outright atheist. Traditionally in philosophy of religion, the predominant worldviews under consideration are theism, which is inherently religious, and naturalism, which is nonreligious or secular. These diametrically opposed worldviews come in many varieties, but here is a rough understanding of their central commitments:

> *Theistic worldviews*: There is a God, or divine mind, worthy of worship and adoration who created and causally interacts with the world, and the ultimate good for human beings can be received by establishing a proper relationship with this divine reality.[5]
>
> *Naturalistic worldviews*: There is no God, gods, or other supernatural entities like spirits, angels, and ghosts. The only causal entities and properties that exist are natural and, in principle, detectable by science.[6]

The most common understanding of God in theistic worldviews is Perfect Being Theism according to which God is a metaphysically perfect being with great-making properties like perfect goodness, omnipotence, and omniscience. Two examples of Naturalistic worldviews would be Scientism (or Scientific Naturalism) and Secular Humanism (see Stenmark 2022a).

An important task among philosophers of religion is the critical assessment of the contents of worldviews, a task which arises from the broad epistemic norm that one should commit to true propositions only. While historically the focus has been on the rationality of belief in the God of theism, it is important to see that *all* worldviews are subject to what we might call *The Rational Feasibility Challenge*:

> The Rational Feasibility Challenge concerns evaluating worldviews by assessing their coherence, consistency, and justification. It primarily involves scrutinising the core commitments of worldviews and their adherence to public evidence. Meeting the challenge means demonstrating that a certain worldview is coherent with the demands of reason.

However, rational feasibility is not the only thing that matters. Worldviews also need to be practically and existentially feasible. They serve not only the theoretical function of structuring reality and making it intelligible, but also a practical or existential function by providing its adherents with guidance and principles to live by. Mikael Stenmark writes: 'A [worldview] actually leads people in how they should lead their lives, how to get through obstacles that

---

[5] Compare with e.g. Stenmark (2022b: 574). [6] Compare with e.g. Oppy (2013: 128).

block the road of ultimate wellbeing. (Or if the [worldview] denies the possibility of ultimate wellbeing, to give guidance about what else to do)' (Stenmark 1995: 243).

Theistic worldviews are often scrutinised for epistemic reasons. Critics worry that they might be irrational or lacking in evidential support. Naturalistic worldviews, on the other hand, more often face the more practical existential challenge. It is questioned whether they are viable options for guiding our lives.

One such challenge for naturalism comes from Thomas Nagel. He asks whether there is anything within naturalistic worldviews capable of fulfilling what he calls our yearning for 'cosmic reconciliation'. He writes:

> Without God, it is unclear what we should aspire to harmony with. But still, the aspiration can remain, to live not merely the life of the creature one is, but in some sense to participate through it in the life of the universe as a whole. To be gripped by this desire is what I mean by the religious temperament. (Nagel 2010: 6)

Not all Nones have the sort of 'religious temperament' that Nagel speaks of here, but some do. Some are gripped by a sort of desire to live in harmony with the universe and not just as an individual in it. For them the cosmic question of 'how to bring into one's individual life a recognition of one's relation to the universe as a whole, whatever that relationship is' (see Nagel 2010: 5) is of great existential significance.

Philip Kitcher states this existential challenge for naturalistic worldviews, claiming that it arises 'initially from skepticism that anything can make good the losses [of meaning and value] it [i.e. naturalism] entails' (Kitcher 2011: 33). The loss for naturalistic worldviews Kitcher mentions is the loss of value and meaning associated with the rejection of God. Kitcher explicates the challenge further by stating that religion can meet certain existential needs like hope and security:

> For people whose lives are going badly, or that are in constant danger of going badly, religion can provide important forms of security, sometimes hope that the reversals of this life will be compensated in the next, and opportunities for mutual consolation. Part of this promise (the idea that the bad things that actually occur will somehow be redeemed) is not easily replicable in a secular framework. (Kitcher 2011: 34)[7]

---

[7] It is not entirely uncontroversial to claim that theistic worldviews manage to secure the values that Kitcher mentions. Some argue that the axiological value of naturalism is greater than that of theism (see Kahane 2011; Lougheed 2020; Penner 2015) and that we should hope for the nonexistence of God. For some examples from this debate together with the introduction of a research programme about how to develop concepts of God based on axiological considerations,

Nagel and Kitcher point at an important challenge worth considering when evaluating any worldview. Call it *The Existential Feasibility Challenge*:

> The Existential Feasibility Challenge concerns the evaluation of a worldview's capacity to guide our lives, both in our day-to-day affairs and on the grand scale, towards alignment with the deepest levels of existence. It also concerns assessing its resources for coping with hardship and existential issues such as meaning and purpose.

While the former challenge is epistemological, the latter is existential and centred on the worldview's ability to guide our lives. A large part of this Element is dedicated to evaluating how Somethingism (spelled out and defined in Section 2), as the ontological component in the worldviews of many Nones, holds up against these challenges (Section 3 concerns the epistemic challenge and Section 4 the existential). But before we start with the philosophical analysis, let us take a closer look at the semi-secular landscape.

1.2 The Worldviews of the Nones

Despite what the word 'None' might seem to suggest, and in accordance with our definition of worldviews as not necessarily being comprehensive, religious Nones also have worldviews. They hold views about say ontology, axiology, epistemology, or praxeology. However, particularly among the Nones, worldviews differ among individuals and are not constrained by institutionalised structures. Instead, a salient feature of the worldviews among these individuals is an opposition to external authorities and a turn towards individualism and – borrowing a term from Paul Heelas and Linda Woodhead – 'subjective spirituality'.[8] Such spirituality sacralises a subjective life, which Heelas and Woodhead explicate as having 'to do with states of consciousness, states of mind, memories, emotions, passions, sensations, bodily experiences, dreams, feelings, inner consciousness, and sentiments – including moral sentiments like compassion' (Heelas & Woodhead 2005: 4).

Perhaps most importantly, they state that 'the subjectivities of each individual become a, if not the, unique source of significance, meaning and authority' (Heelas & Woodhead 2005: 4). Referring to their study of spirituality in the British town of Kendal, Heelas and Woodhead observe that the authentic life of

---

see Jonbäck (2022). According to Schellenberg (2019a: 17–33), this whole debate is seriously confused since theism entails the existence of the highest possible good, and any rejection of its value must therefore build on misunderstanding.

[8] Indeed, many scholars understand this 'subjective turn' as a defining feature of Western culture. (See, for example, Davie 1994; Heelas & Woodhead 2005; Taylor 1989; 1991; 2002.)

the individual is pursued not so much through institutionalised religion, but rather through a broad spectrum of practices that fit within a 'holistic milieu'. Such practices include, among others, yoga, circle dancing, meditation, reiki, and homeopathy. Heelas and Woodhead found that many Nones could not find anything that could fulfill their spiritual yearning in a congregational (Christian or Jewish) setting, which is why they turn to exploring the holistic milieu. Here are some examples:

> A one hour service on Sunday? I mean it's not really enough time to address your self-esteem issue is it! ... I didn't find any help in the churches ... I find it in a Twelve Step Program ... *That* was the start of my personal journey. (Heelas & Woodhead 2005: 122)

> I didn't see my Christian upbringing as being spiritual ... It was only when I began Transcendental Meditation ... that I found the spirituality I wanted ... the spirituality within each person. (Heelas and Woodhead 2005: 122)

The subjective turn, particularly in the West, was acknowledged already in the early 1990s by Charles Taylor (1991: 26) who presented it as the 'massive subjective turn of modern culture'. What might be called *new spirituality* practices now have a strong presence throughout the Western world.

In her seminal *Strange Rites*, Tara Isabella Burton describes many American Nones as religiously remixed. This broad subgroup 'envision themselves as creators of their own bespoke religions, mixing and matching, spiritual and aesthetic and experiential and philosophical traditions' (Burton 2020: 10). The diversity of views among the remixed is remarkable. Burton's exposé includes a mixture of views derived from, for example, Harry Potter fandom, wellness culture, witchcraft, and techno-utopianism. Like the Nones in Kendal, a common feature among the remixed is the rejection of authority and institution, in favour of personal choice and individual experience.

Burton's presentation of what she calls the theology of wellness culture illustrates what can almost be described as a sacralisation of subjective experience. This theology is one of the divisions between 'the authentic, intuitional self – both body and soul – and the artificial, malevolent forces of society, rules, and expectations' (Burton 2020: 94). She clarifies further:

> We are born good, but we are tricked, by Big Pharma, processed food, by civilization itself, into living something that falls short of our best life. Our sins, if they exist at all, lie in insufficient self-attention or self-care: false modesty, undeserved humilities, refusing to shine bright ... We have to listen to ourselves, to behave authentically, in tune with what our intuition dictates. (Burton 2020: 94)

The remixing of ideas and rejection of traditional authorities in favour of subjective experience in fact reaches beyond the Nones. Burton demonstrates how many people who do not identify as Nones share these patterns. She calls this group the 'religious hybrids': 'People who say they belong to a given religion, and believe or practice a portion of it. But they also feel free to disregard elements that don't necessarily suit them, or to supplement their official practice with spiritual or ritualistic elements, not to mention beliefs, from other traditions' (Burton 2020: 22).

Burton explains that about 60 per cent of all Nones (i.e. including the fully secularised) believe in at least one of the following phenomena: astrology, psychics, spiritual energy in physical objects, or reincarnation. According to Burton, an identical percentage of Christians in the United States believe in at least one of the same phenomena (Burton 2020: 22).

Many of the Nones not only combine different practices and elements to make their homemade worldview. They are also 'spiritually fluid', not staying with one combination of worldview components for long. Instead, they let their curiosity guide them to explore other options (Burton 2020: 23). This is coherent with an observation from Linda Mercadante that many Nones are not 'seekers' in the traditional sense, but what she calls 'explorers'. This means that they are not looking for a new spiritual home, but are content with constantly moving between ideas, reworking their worldviews as they go along (Mercadante 2014: 58–60). Some of these explorers are even explicit in their embrace of syncretism: ' My religious identification right now would be that of a religious syncretist. I'm taking bits and pieces of my own path, my own world and experience' (Mercadante 2014: 173).

This far, we have observed a strong emphasis on individualism among the Nones, along with a blend of spiritual practices. Additionally, when considering the epistemological components of their worldviews, we find that many Nones, particularly the semi-secular, seem to regard experience and intuition as the main reliable source of knowledge. We have also seen that many Nones mix and match from different traditions, reincarnation, karma, astrology, yoga, and reiki being some examples. But what about belief in God and the transcendent?

According to the Pew Research Center (2024), about 70 per cent of the Nones believe in, if not God, at least a higher power or that 'there is something spiritual beyond the natural world'. However, statistical studies do not reveal much detail. To quarry deeper into what the Nones mean when they say they believe in something spiritual beyond or a higher power, Mercadante conducted a large interview study with Nones in the United States who identify as spiritual but not religious. When exploring what her interviewees meant by their belief in something like God or something sacred she writes that:

> I soon learned I could not assume that when they spoke of the "sacred", a transcendent reality, a divine dimension, or even used the word "God", that they meant a "personal" God, an "Almighty" who created the world, hears prayers, takes an active part in earthly affairs, and – even if an eternal non-bodily Presence – is nevertheless someone with whom they can "have a relationship". (Mercadante 2014: 93)

Even though the interviews conducted showed that the 'something' informants believed existed was, as Mercadante presents it, 'usually greater than their individual selves', the idea that the spiritual and not religious are so-called believers without belonging is not correct either. While many had some view about something transcendent, it differed from a traditional concept of God in varying degrees (Mercadante 2014: 93–94).

A clear tendency in the interviews was the elimination of descriptive details from the God of their often-Christian upbringing. Mercadante describes how her informant 'Amy' has reworked her conception of God. According to 'Amy' her 'Sunday school version [of God] has always been, you know, the Wizard of Oz running the show', and Mercadante continues that 'now – as many interviewees did – she has stripped away both masculine and personal imagery, seeing God more as a "metaphysical non-embodied entity beyond definition"' (Mercadante 2014: 98).

Another tendency in the same vein highlighted in Mercadante's study is a rejection of the word 'God' because of its interventionist connotations. The interviewee and former Catholic Ricco explains:

> I don't like the word God because it's too loaded ... Although ... I do believe that there is something that is, that we are all connected to ... something bigger than us ... [But is this] something outside of us, controlling what we're doing? No. Not into it, not down with it. (Mercadante 2014: 99)

Some deviated even more from a traditional personal concept of God. The interviewee Connie explains:

> I have trouble with the concept of God. But if you talk about a universal presence or a resonating energy at a certain frequency, the result of that is quietude or peace or harmonics within you are quieted. I get that resonating harmonic when I am doing self-growth and self-knowledge work and I don't think I need God to do that. (Mercadante 2014: 107)

These increasingly vague, or perhaps general attitudes towards something transcendent, be it God or a higher power of a general presence, are not unique for American Nones. In fact, the tendency towards more abstract and vague notions of the transcendent are even more prevalent in the European context.

1.3 Somethingism

European scholars have coined the term 'Somethingism' to describe the sort of vague and abstract beliefs about the divine that many Nones give expression to, a term literally meaning belief in something. It was first used in the Netherlands, where already in 2005 almost 40 per cent of the population would subscribe to what they call 'Ietsism' (the Dutch term for Somethingism (Couwenberg 2005)). Similar numbers have been reported in the Czech Republic, where the native term in Czech is 'Něcismus' (Berglund 2018: 1). For a fuller description of how European Somethingism can be expressed, we turn to our (i.e. the authors') home country of Sweden, which is often considered the most secular country in the world.

According to Pippa Norris and Ronald Inglehart's *World Culture Map*, which is based on data from the *World Values Survey*, Sweden is on top when it comes to how strongly rooted secular views and values are in the population at large. Such values, common among the Nones everywhere, include values like individual self-expression and personal happiness. It also includes rejecting the idea of a personal God at the individual level, that is, the idea of a personal God does not have any great significance for their personal lives.[9]

While it is certainly the case that belief in a personal God is lacking among most Swedes, there are not many full-blown naturalists in Sweden either. Instead, most Swedes are semi-secular, situated somewhere in between a naturalistic and a theistic worldview. Swedish sociologist Erika Willander approximates that the semi-secular Nones now make up the majority of the Swedish population:

> Only five percent of the Swedish population can be categorized as fully religious. The rest cannot, however, be analyzed as fully non-religious as only about 20 percent of the population say that they do not believe in any God or supernatural power ... These numbers suggest that most people in Sweden, approximately 75 percent, can be thought of as neither fully religious nor fully unreligious. (Willander 2020: 37–38)

---

[9] See the *World Culture Map* and the discussion in Willander (2015). Scholars like Phil Zuckerman (2009: 57) depict Sweden as 'about as secular as sociologically possible' and make this judgement by focusing on a widespread lack of traditional Christian beliefs and low numbers of traditional religious practitioners in the country.

Among the Swedish Nones, we find a diversity of individualistic perspectives including eclectic or so-called homemade views, subjects simultaneously ascribing to supernatural and naturalistic interpretations of the same life-changing events (Burén 2015). Most notably, however, is a variety of vague beliefs in 'something' more or less unspecified. The religious historian David Thurfjell notes the prevalence of this latter belief in 'something' among the Swedes:[10]

> Swedes largely express a sceptical attitude towards religion in general, and a mildly critical attitude towards religion is common in public discourse. However, many adopt a faith-based stance that can be described as ambivalent. It is characterized for the majority not by atheism but by a personal belief in a vague "something". (Thurfjell 2015: 28–29)[11]

To get a somewhat clearer view of the diversity of Somethingism in Sweden we can look at two interesting examples from two different studies. As an epigraph in a study by Willander, we get the paradigmatic example Gunilla, who explains that:

> I cannot say that I am really "Christian" or religious, but I do believe in something which is not only physical. Well, maybe not a God but that there is something . . . that there is goodness in the world . . . well, it would be hard to live without that, I believe. (Willander 2020: 64)

Gunilla qualifies her thought about this 'something' by saying that it is 'not only physical' while others from the same study present it as 'something beyond humans' and yet others lean more heavily towards classical agnosticism and suggest that this 'something . . . may be God or may be something else' (Willander 2020: 66). Willander also discovered that this 'something', to which many of her informants appeal, often is described as having axiological qualities; it is a 'higher goodness' or a 'sense of justice' (Willander 2020: 66). In the quote from Gunilla this goodness is also of significant importance, which is indicated by the sentence 'it would be hard to live without that, I believe'.

In another study by Thurfjell, concerning the belief and practices of the many Swedes who have their most significant experiences while being alone in the forest, it becomes clear that many lack words to describe what they experience and believe. One example would be Per, who says that there is something in the

---

[10] Perhaps sensing how common this vague belief in something is, the programme *Människor och tro* (people and their faith) on Swedish national radio in 2017, following the Netherlands and the Czech Republic, coined the word 'Nåtism' (a direct translation of 'Somethingism' into Swedish) and introduced it together with the question of whether Somethingism rather than traditional Christianity constitutes Sweden's new main religion.

[11] Our own translation. For Swedish sources, all translations are ours unless otherwise stated.

forest 'besides everything else' and goes on to state that 'I've never bothered to try to explain it ... it fulfills certain functions ... a security, but, but also cognitively something rational ... that it is something that ... well it is difficult'. Per goes on to explain where he gets into contact with this 'something' and says:

> Maybe it's when I'm out running, then I stop ... it's become a bit of a habit ... I stop. There is a particularly beautiful place in a small wooded area over there, and I stand there for a few minutes ... Then it doesn't become this usual inner dialogue, it becomes a dialogue with "something". (Thurfjell 2020: 213)

Thurfjell points out that like Per, many Nones who lack words to describe what they believe or come in contact with are satisfied with being vague. Many think that preciseness would tarnish their experience, making it less meaningful for them (Thurfjell 2020: 222).

Sweden is an interesting example due to its far-gone secularisation, but as should be clear, it is by no means the only country where these vague beliefs in something are present. We find more or less explicit Somethingism in many other European countries,[12] and it clearly resonates well with the views on the transcendent prevalent among American Nones. Our understanding of Somethingism is that it is more than simply one view among others in the multifaceted semi-secular landscape of the Nones. Of course, not all Nones subscribe to Somethingism, and such homogeneity should anyhow not be expected from the Nones, but enough Nones do accept Somethingism for it to be possible to view this vague and general view as a kind of common denominator. More to the point: if anything unites the disparate Nones, it is the belief in 'something'.

At this point, it might be worthwhile to return to the worldview framework. The ontological component of a worldview is the part which tells us what ultimately exists. In theism, this is God. In naturalism, it is matter and energy. Given the fact that Somethingism in some sense concerns the deepest level of reality, it makes considerable sense to regard Somethingism as the ontological component of the worldviews of the Nones, or at the very least, as the most distinguished and existentially important aspect of the Nones ontology. It is this understanding which has prompted us to dedicate this rather exploratory Element on the worldviews of the Nones to Somethingism. It is on this understanding we now proceed in our efforts to make philosophical sense of this often vague and curiously abstract view.

---

[12] See, for example, Thurfjell et al. (2019). For a short overview of Sweden, see Jonbäck and Palmqvist (2024).

A preliminary before continuing. While there has not been much, if any, philosophical work on Somethingism itself, similar general religious views have been explored at length by John L. Schellenberg. In earlier writing Schellenberg (2009; 2013) defended Ultimism, the view that there exists a metaphysically, soteriologically, and axiologically ultimate reality. In later writings, he has mainly concerned himself with the weaker view that a metaphysically, soteriologically, and axiologically transcendent reality exists (Schellenberg 2019b). Since our analysis of Somethingism will place it very close to the latter view (in fact, we will argue that the latter view is a kind of Somethingism), Schellenberg will constitute our main discussion partner throughout this Element.

1.4 The Structure of the Element

The actual views of the Nones are often half-articulated at best. In order to subject Somethingism to philosophical scrutiny, we first need to make a rational reconstruction of its core content, along with the main varieties we encounter among the Nones. That is the subject of the upcoming Section 2.

Section 3 concerns the epistemological challenge. It concerns not only the basic issue of whether it is rational to believe in Somethingism, but also deeper issues, such as the methods the Nones use in their intellectual journey from a detailed, religious view to abstract claims. In what sense is this a rational process? We also consider the relationship between Somethingism and non-doxasticism, the currently popular idea in philosophy of religion that our attitude towards the central propositions of our worldviews need not be one of belief, but rather hope or acceptance.

The existential challenge is the focus of Section 4. It concerns three interconnected questions. First, if Somethingism is true, does it offer the Nones what they need to live in alignment with 'something'? Second, is it possible to live one's life guided by Somethingism, in a manner similar to how religion guides the life of the traditional believer? Third, does Somethingism have the resources necessary to cope with existential problems, such as the problem of evil?

The element ends with a short conclusive section, where the results are summarised along with some brief suggestions regarding possible future avenues of research.

2 Towards a Philosophical Understanding of Somethingism

In this section, we attempt to pin down what it could mean when the None report that 'I believe in something'. We begin by offering a philosophical understanding of Somethingism, in relation to some recent accounts (Elliott 2017; Gan

Semi-Secular Worldviews and the Belief in Something Beyond

2022; Leech 2020; Schellenberg 2019a).[13] It is not only an attempt to make explicit what is meant by the claim 'something exists', but an attempt to spell out the fuller view it implies.

The philosophical understanding we aim at offers a much-elaborated picture as compared to what the Nones are actually saying. Going beyond the actual sources would have been problematic on a more empirical approach. However, as philosophers, our main task is not to correctly retell the views of individual subjects, but to explore the philosophical implications of what is said, and assess the underlying philosophical views. This is no more strange than when other philosophers of religion discuss abstract views about God, such as perfect being theism or process theism, regardless of whether these views are what individual religious theists actually believe in.

After clarifying the philosophical tenets of Somethingism we offer a preliminary taxonomy in which we distinguish between some important varieties of Somethingism which are prevalent in the empirical material.

2.1 Characterising Somethingism

As the empirical material makes clear, the primary context in which Nones report that 'I believe in something' is when they talk about the existence of God. This is important since it teaches us at least three things about Somethingism.

Firstly, it seems that the somethingist is eager to distinguish her own view from a traditional Christian worldview and traditional belief in God (understood according to perfect being theism).[14] Otherwise, she would presumably just have answered the question 'Do you believe in God' with a 'Yes'.[15] This is a point worth keeping in mind since many formulations of Somethingism are in fact so general that they do not logically exclude perfect being theism. When Nones say that they believe in a higher power, higher justice, or a certain goodness they arguably mean a goodness or higher justice which is not God, even though the truth conditions for the axiological quality they allude to would be satisfied if God existed. A clear example would be Gunilla from the previous section:

---

[13] Most philosophers use the Dutch term *Ietsisme* (often with the anglicised spelling *Ietsism*) to describe the position of Somethingism. We use Somethingism to keep in line with the language used by English-speaking Nones. It should also be noted that Somethingism has primarily been of philosophical interest as an alternative to Schellenbergian Ultimism.

[14] Perfect being theism seems to be the view about God shared by most people who do not believe in God. This is easily understandable since perfect being theism has long been the dominant view of God in the West, and since most arguments against the existence of God presupposes this view.

[15] As explained in Section 1, this distancing from both traditional religion and from the God of perfect being theism is common for most if not all Nones.

> I cannot say that I am really "Christian" or religious, but I do believe in something which is not only physical. Well, maybe not a God but that there is something ... that there is goodness in the world ... well, it would be hard to live without that, I believe (Willander 2020: 64).

Secondly, since the somethingist does not answer the question 'Do you believe in God' with a 'No', she seems equally eager to demarcate against some understanding of atheism. It is a bit tricky to pinpoint exactly what she is against. It could not be atheism in the sense of rejecting traditional belief in God, because as we have already seen, the somethingist embraces atheism in that limited sense. However, in everyday language, atheism is often understood as synonymous with a naturalistic worldview. It might seem reasonable to suppose that the 'something' the Nones talk about exists outside the causal world, and that it is naturalism the somethingist demarcates against. However, as will be clear in what follows, there is also conceptual space for a naturalistic Somethingism, and therefore we should be careful not to presuppose that *all* somethingists envisage 'something' as supernatural. What we take all somethingists to reject is therefore not atheism in the sense of a naturalistic worldview, but in the sense that nothing *existentially significant* exists.

This brings us to the third point we can discern from the context in which we primarily find expressions of Somethingism, namely that 'something' is supposed to occupy the central stage held by God in a traditional religious worldview. 'Something' must therefore be of major importance, both in itself and in the life of the somethingist. This is explicit when Gunilla states about her belief in something that 'it would be hard to live without that, I believe'. In other words, 'something' is the existentially significant worldview component which makes it impossible for the somethingist to simply say no when asked whether she believes in God. Borrowing a term from Peter Gan, we can therefore characterise 'something' as Truly Significant Being (TSB):

> There are indeed as many ways of being religious or spiritual as there are people who seriously commit themselves to what they think is a Truly Significant Being (TSB) – principle, value, way of life, or substantive being. (Gan 2022: 171)

According to Gan, a TSB is something tremendously important which exists as a suitable object for serious commitment. We agree, but we think that one dimension is missing, namely that making the commitment should have a significant impact on one's life. As suggested by Schellenberg, an existentially significant object also needs to be 'importantly life-enhancing for those who respond properly to it' (Schellenberg 2019a: 160–161). Therefore, when we talk about TSB in what follows, we think of it as including this life-enhancing aspect. Beyond that, we do not wish to add any more details to the characterisation of TSB – it is important to keep the object of Somethingism as general and vague as possible.

Truly Significant Being does not have to be supernatural, but it cannot be completely ordinary either. Ordinary things can be truly significant and life-enhancing, like one's spouse or one's home, but they are not proper objects for any spirituality or religious life. It would be absurd to suggest that a None who says she believes in 'something' might refer to her husband. As observed by Schellenberg, when the Nones say they believe in 'something', they usually mean that they believe in 'something more', something beyond everyday existence (Schellenberg 2019a: 159). Schellenberg suggests that we use the term 'transmundane' to describe that which lies beyond the ordinary without being supernatural:

> The mundane in one sense – the sense relevant here – is the ordinary or the everyday, what all of us encounter by doing such things as eating and sleeping and brushing our teeth and going to work ... Transmundane realities, as we might call them, are found in many and various departments of human life, science and philosophy and art among them. (Schellenberg 2019a: 159–160)

Of course, there is much which is transmundane in this sense without being a proper TSB, like weird art, or meaningless out-of-the-ordinary experiences, like *déja vu* or fever hallucinations.[16] But the suggestion is only that being transmundane is a necessary condition for TSB, not that it is also sufficient or that the categories are co-extensive.

In the concept of a transmundane TSB, we have identified a minimal understanding of the 'something' many Nones report believing in. It is minimal in the sense that transmundanity represents the most modest way in which something might exist beyond everyday experience. Let us call this minimal form Weak Somethingism.

Weak Somethingism: A transmundane TSB exists.

The encounter with something significant and transmundane in this week sense aligns closely with the inner-life spirituality discussed by Heelas and Woodhead in their study on the subjective turn (Heelas & Woodhead: 2005). It also

---

[16] Interestingly, what is transmundane seems to vary between cultural contexts, since parts of life we do not normally talk about or treat with an out-of-sight, out-of-mind policy tend to become transmundane with the passing of time. For example, in current Western culture it does not seem far-fetched to suggest that death has been so far removed from everyday life that experiences with death have become transmundane. The Victorians arguably did the same thing with sex, and it is far from obvious that Western culture has yet normalised sexual experience. For a treatment of contemporary sexual phenomena as having spiritual and arguably transmundane qualities, see Burton (2020: ch. 7).

resonates with the experiences and nihilistic beliefs exhibited in wellness culture, that is through modern self-care practices such as meditation, diet, and rigorous exercise (Burton 2020: 91–114).

However, many Nones seem to have something stronger in mind when they talk about 'something more'. Often it presented as a higher power, justice or spiritual force distinct from what is described by traditional religion. For example, a majority of the Nones in America report this type of beliefs (Burton 2020: 17). Also, when interviewees in Sweden explicates their belief in 'something' by appealing to 'something beyond humans' (Willander 2020: 65) it is clear that what they talk about does not only go beyond our everyday life, but also beyond the natural world. In short, their worldview does not only contain transmundane phenomena but supernatural, or, as we will refer to them to keep in line with current literature, transcendent phenomena.[17]

It should be noted that even though transmundane ideas are generally more low-key and less fantastical than transcendent, this does not necessarily have to be the case. On certain transmundane worldviews, natural reality can be quite fantastical. Think, for example, of simulation theory, which posits that we all live in a powerful computer simulation. If such a theory is true, many phenomena which would be supernatural on the traditional scientific realist picture would be natural, like gods (the software engineers responsible for running the simulation), an afterlife (a re-boot? copy-paste? the possibilities are endless) or, confusingly enough, transcendent reality itself (if we are in a simulation, the real world is transcendent reality to us).[18] However, it seems obvious that the vast majority of Nones who are careful to point out that the 'something' they believe in is naturalistic (or 'scientific', 'logical', or 'materialistic', which are the words people commonly use when they mean 'naturalistic') do not consider such extravagant possibilities.

When it comes to religion, philosophers usually distinguish between three relevant kinds of transcendence: metaphysical, axiological, and soteriological. Metaphysical transcendency concerns the deep structure of reality, and transcendent metaphysical truths are more fundamental facts about the world than the ones found in the natural world. Axiological transcendency is about having

---

[17] Note that in defining 'transcendent' as 'beyond the world as described by science', we get a notion of transcendency which is relative to the current scientific worldview. It is in an important way contemporary, since future scientific progress might lead to a different division between what is scientific and what is supernatural. However, this is still preferable over defining transcendence as forever beyond the grasp of science, because who knows how science might develop in the deep future?

[18] For the most prominent defender of simulation theory (according to which it is has roughly 40 per cent chance of being true), see Bostrom (2003). For a thorough discussion on how simulation theory makes traditional religious and supernatural ideas feasible, see Steinhart (2014).

a value which is greater than any purely natural thing. Soteriological transcendency concerns a higher human good, better than any natural human good (Schellenberg 2019a: 165).

James Elliott (2017) has identified Somethingism with the claim that a soteriologically transcendent reality exists, and he thinks that the somethingist should be agnostic whether this reality is transcendent in the other two aspects:[19]

> [Somethingism]: There exists a soteriologically transcendent reality that may or may not also be axiologically and/or metaphysically transcendent (and very little more can be said regarding its nature). (Elliott 2017: 98)

Elliott certainly has a point, since it is hard to see how a transcendent something could be a religiously relevant TSB without being soteriologically transcendent. At the same time, it seems equally obvious that a metaphysically and axiologically transcendent reality which lacks soteriological transcendency (i.e., something most valuable existing beyond nature from which we could hope to gain nothing, like a deity indifferent to all life) would not be a suitable TSB. Therefore, it might seem natural to conclude that only soteriological transcendency is needed.

However, as pointed out by David Leech, it seems questionable that there can be a soteriologically transcendent reality which is not also metaphysically transcendent, because it seems intuitive that a transcendent good can only be achieved in relation to a transcendent object, that is, in relation to something metaphysically transcendent (Leech 2020: 123–124). We agree with Leech, since we find it hard to see how a human good from a natural source could ever in itself be considered transcendent. It seems to be part of the very concept of a natural explanation, that that which can be explained by natural causes is itself a natural phenomenon, and so we cannot see how soteriological transcendency can exist except with a metaphysical source.

One does not even have to consider the source of soteriological transcendency to see that it requires metaphysical transcendency. Soteriological transcendency requires metaphysical transcendency by definition. If a soteriologically transcendent reality exists, reality has a deeper structure than the natural world alone, and its existence would therefore be a metaphysical fact. It is perhaps telling that Elliott offers no concrete examples to illustrate what a soteriologically transcendent reality without metaphysical transcendence could look like.

---

[19] It should be noted that Elliott is not interested in working out Somethingism as a reasonable position, as much as arguing for the fact that commitment to a soteriological transcendency only is the most general (and therefore most likely and most preferable) religious stance available. His aim is to challenge Schellenberg's claim that we should prefer simple ultimism.

Does the transcendent also need to have axiological qualities to be the source of the greatest human good? It seems clear to us that in a strict, logical sense it does not. While soteriological transcendency logically requires metaphysical transcendency, no such connection exists between soteriological and axiological transcendency. A soteriologically transcendent reality might lack any intrinsic value, and only have instrumental value as a means of delivering the ultimate human good.

However, as Schellenberg (2005; 2009; 2019b) has often reminded us, all major religious worldviews we know of today encompass all three kinds of transcendence. He suggests that the notion of axiological transcendency should be included in a transcendent version of Somethingism to make justice to our religious emotions:

> A transcendent religious reality would be greater in *inherent value* than anything in nature. To do justice to religious emotions we have to say that it would rightly be attractive to us in a way that is captured by speaking of inherent value. (Schellenberg 2019a: 165, italics in original)

What Schellenberg seems to be getting at here is that we have a deeply seated intuition that a proper religious object must be inherently valuable. This also seems in line with the notion of TSB employed so far, since it seems natural to suggest that a truly significant being must be highly important in its own right and not just as a means to an end. Especially since TSB is supposed to replace God as the existentially significant part of the somethingist's worldview.

The point that a proper, transcendent TSB requires an axiological side can be illustrated by a thought experiment. Envision a soteriological and metaphysical transcendent without axiological qualities. To keep in line with Western religious tradition, suppose that this transcendent entity is also a person. Had it had axiological qualities, it would have been a deity, but now it is just a valueless transcendent person with the key to our greatest good. Not only would this entity not be worthy of worship, but there would be nothing incorrect in tricking or manipulating or even torturing it to give us the greatest human good. Since the entity lacks any intrinsic value, we could treat it worse than we ever would another human. Sure, control over the entity might be our most prized resource, but it would be strange to think of it as a TSB. Some would even argue that if we have a manipulative and controlling relation to the source of our greatest good, we are no longer religious but practitioners of magic and perhaps even demonology.

Add axiological transcendency and everything changes. The entity is now more important than anything in the natural world and mistreating it would be the worst possible offense. With axiological transcendency, the entity is a proper deity and a TSB.

With these considerations in mind, it seems natural to suggest that the strong, supernatural form of Somethingism should include triple transcendency.

> **Strong Somethingism:** A TSB exists which is soteriologically, metaphysically, and axiologically transcendent.

Perhaps it might be objected that in formulating Strong Somethingism, we have been overly occupied with traditional religion. As we have seen, the Nones are religious individualists, and many take their own well-being as an indicator of truth and as an important religious and spiritual goal in itself (Mercadante 2014, Burton 2020: 107) Perhaps it would not be strange if these Nones were to blur the border between magic and religion when trying out 'what works for me', and perhaps they would not dismiss the idea of a transcendent reality with only instrumental value? While this might well be the case, we would like to point out two things. First, it seems that the personal well-being which is important to Nones is of a natural rather than a supernatural kind, and it therefore seems more relevant in relation to Weak Somethingism. Secondly, we already have a notion of Somethingism which includes all instances, namely Weak Somethingism (remember that everything which is transcendent is also per definition transmundane). In formulating Strong Somethingism, we seek the most substantial view discernible from the idea that 'something exists', and that seems to be the idea of a triple transcendence. The fact that there might be weaker forms of Somethingism which are still transcendent is, of course, interesting, but it should not lead us to reconsider the formulation of Strong Somethingism.

Another possible objection, perhaps a bit more theological in nature, comes from advocates of the distinction between a transcendent and an immanent supernatural. In this tradition, the transcendent is seen as more distant from the natural world, while the immanent in some sense resides within the natural world.

To explain why we reject the idea of immanency, we must first clarify the concept. Immanency can mean at least two things. Radical immanency is the view that the 'supernatural' literally resides in the world, like the ancient Greek pagans thought their gods lived on top of Mount Olympus. On modest immanency, the supernatural is not part of the world described by science, but it exists in close relation to it. On this view, an animist tree spirit does not literally live in a tree. It is somehow tied to a tree, but it dwells on another plane of existence, beyond the world of our senses.

While radical immanency was the default view of the divine for ancient pagans and medieval Christians alike, the idea is becoming increasingly untenable in our secularised and disenchanted world. Charles Taylor has described this by saying that the immanent frame of our current worldview is closed, and that the only possible religious options left are the transcendent (Taylor 2007: 529–549). As pointed out by Palmqvist (2023: 660–662), given the scientific picture of the natural world, there is simply no room for anything supernatural to exist within it.[20] The natural world has been thoroughly explored, and it is hard to even imagine how anything supernatural could exist within it. We have checked the summit of Mount Olympus, and it was empty. The only place where the supernatural can reside is outside the natural world.

Since modest immanency does not claim that anything supernatural resides in the world, it is not problematic in the same way as its radical counterpart. However, what is modestly immanent is by definition also transcendent, since it is supernatural and beyond the natural world, making the immanent a sub-category of the transcendent. On such a picture, the only difference between immanence and proper transcendence is how 'far' beyond the natural world we conceive of it. Here, we must remember that distances (for all we know) only exist in the natural world, and that all talk of 'distance' beyond the natural world is highly metaphorical, which makes the distinction itself metaphorical. Since the interpretative possibilities are almost endless when it comes to metaphors, this obfuscates the distinction to uselessness. Any attempt to solve the problem by stipulating a fixed border between immanence and transcendence would only be arbitrary, and therefore the most straightforward way to handle the problem is to make do without immanency.

2.2 Varieties of Qualified Somethingism

The most striking feature of Somethingism is that the view is abstract and vague rather than concrete and specific. Compared with traditional religious views, there is a significant lack of detail. We can say that Somethingism is characterised by its 'thin content'.

While there are certainly Nones who only claim to believe in 'something' while refusing to give any further description, most are a bit more forthcoming. They qualify the view that 'something exists' by giving some vague examples,

---

[20] This, of course, is on the assumption that scientific realism is correct. If anti-realism is correct and our scientific theories are not literally true or close to the truth, who knows what might exist in the world.

or add some important detail, or specify the context or epistemic background of their view. We must therefore distinguish between those who only accept Somethingism in its barest forms (i.e. Weak Somethingism or Strong Somethingism only), and those who expand on the view, if only in the slightest. The views of the latter still have a very thin content as compared to traditional alternatives, but they are not as thin as the views of the former. Let us call the first kind Pure Somethingism, and the latter Qualified Somethingism. In this subsection, we explore some important varieties of Qualified Somethingism.

Of course, there are presumably as many versions of qualified Somethingism as there are somethingists going beyond the pure versions.[21] The Nones are notoriously individualistic when constructing their worldviews, and with each making her own additions to 'something', the resulting pictures are varied to say the least. To keep it manageable, we make a distinction between three types of Qualified Somethingism. We call them 'Old Religion Somethingism', 'New Spirituality Somethingism', and 'Life Question Somethingism'. In relation to these types, we also identify three different reasons for turning to a view with thin content. These types and reasons are ideal types in the Weberian sense, and we expect that many if not most somethingists hold views which combine them. Nonetheless, we think that putting them side by side like this brings clarity to the discussion.

Old Religion Somethingism

Sometimes, the ties between Somethingism and traditional religion are easy to detect. When 'something' is conceptualised as 'something bigger than us' or 'a force on the side of life' by a None with connections to a Christian congregation, it is not far-fetched to think of this 'something' as a vaguer version of God. Mercadante's interviewee and former Catholic, Ricci from the previous section, who rejects the word 'God', but still reports that he believes 'that there is something that is, that we are all connected to ... something bigger than us' would be a relevant example of this thinned belief (Mercadante 2014: 99). On the other hand, when a self-identified None with a heavy interest in Buddhist meditation claims to believe 'in something, a kind of higher justice', it is not implausible to read this 'something' as closely related to karmic principles, although expressed in a less concrete fashion (of course, if Rico had made the same claims, we would naturally have thought of 'a kind of higher justice' as

---

[21] See, for example, Mercadante (2014: ch. 5) where she explicitly tries to dig deeper into what her respondents meant when they reported that they 'believed in Something'. The findings reveal an intriguing palette of still somewhat vague views. However, respondents are often concrete when explicating which traditional religious beliefs they neglect.

God's justice). Obviously, not all instances where the 'something' of Somethingism can be considered an abstract version of the more robust claims of traditional religion are as easily identifiable as in these examples, or as easy to trace back to their source. Nonetheless, it seems that a sizeable portion of the somethingists adhere to what we call 'Old Religion Somethingism'. This type of Somethingism is the vague sibling of traditional religion, defined by the fact that its TSB is an abstract and vague redescription of a traditional religious TSB, lacking in concrete details:

> **Old Religion Somethingism**: A transcendent TSB exists which is described without much detail, but with obvious similarity to the TSB of some traditional religion.

A striking feature of Old Religion Somethingism is the process in which the concrete claims of traditional religion are thinned out and replaced by more abstract counterparts. On the individual level, this process presumably originates in a personal inability to embrace the original claims, be it for moral or epistemic reasons. For example, a None might have a problem with the patriarchal language embedded in Christian tradition, and therefore want to make away with anything she finds problematic, which might be all descriptions of God in anthropomorphic terms, or perhaps even the idea of a personal God itself. She therefore goes through a process of abstraction, until she finds a more general view representing what she perceives to be the abstract core of the claim 'God exists', like 'something more exists, a good lifeforce or something' and which she is able to accept (for real-life examples like this, see Mercadante 2014: 93–125). We call this method of arriving at something acceptable by abstracting away from a more concrete but unacceptable claim 'thinning by reduction of content', and the resultant view is thereby 'thin due to reduction'.

Old Religion Somethingism does not seem to come in a weak form. It is always an instance of Strong Somethingism because of its intimate connection with traditional religion. The TSBs of traditional religions (like God, karmic principles, Dao, Brahman, Buddha Nature, and so forth) are always transcendent, and transcendency does not seem to be among the things left behind in the thinning process. To the contrary, it seems important that the 'something more' must retain its transcendent status, if it is to continue playing roughly the same role as before the 'thinning'. To see this, consider, for example, what a 'something, like a higher justice' could mean interpreted as a transmundane rather than a transcendent idea. A transmundane justice system would be something like the strange court, operating by unknown laws and existing partly outside common society, in which Josef K is prosecuted in Kafka's *The Trial*. Even if Kafka's court existed in real life, it would not be a suitable TSB and it could never play the role of God's justice. A transmundane reading of a 'good force' encounters similar problems (what would a transmundane good force be like? A secret paramilitary vigilante organisation? Something normative in physics?).

New Spirituality Somethingism

Among the Nones (and especially among the Nones of North America), there are many who identify as 'Spiritual But Not Religious'. Even if the expression is a bit problematic in what it denies (on any more qualified definition of religion, most of these Nones would qualify as religious, even though they themselves reject that label), it still tells us a great deal about what is significant for these Nones, namely spirituality.

There are certainly many forms of spirituality in circulation among the Nones, some related to traditional (mostly Eastern) religion, while others are more contemporary inventions. In some of these new forms, like wellness culture, spirituality becomes a lifestyle deeply integrated in a capitalist frame (Burton 2020). Other current forms of spirituality, such as the one based on feelings of interconnectedness with nature, are more about leaving the contemporary world behind, if only for a moment (Thurfjell et al. 2019). And then there are forms which might not be seen as spirituality by their practitioners, but only by interpreting scholars, such as online fandom or online role-playing games (Burton 2020).

The concept of spirituality is multi-faceted and hard to pin down. For example, partaking in a form of spirituality must be distinguished from being a 'spiritual person' since being the latter is clearly possible without doing the former. For present purposes, we think of spirituality as a kind of life-enhancing practice. Doing so, we face the question what distinguishes spirituality from other forms of life-enhancing practices, such as therapy or other non-spiritual forms of self-improvement. Our tentative answer is that spirituality has at least a transmundane and possibly a transcendent dimension. It is a practice which somehow reaches beyond the world of everyday life.

If spirituality is a life-enhancing practice with at least a transmundane dimension, the connection to Somethingism seems obvious. The core of Somethingism is that a TSB which is at least transmundane exists, and which enhances the life of those who commit to it. Therefore, spirituality might be conceptualised simply as a commitment to such a TSB. In its purest or less detailed form, New Spirituality Somethingism is simply lived spirituality in combination with some kinds of Pure Somethingism.

New Spirituality Somethingism: A life-enhancing practice centred on the assumption that a TSB exists which is at least transmundane, and which is described without much detail.

Exactly how to elaborate an understanding of the transmundane (or transcendent) a practitioner has in relation to her spiritual practice varies greatly between subjects. Take yoga as an example. On one hand, we have practitioners who do not want to be reminded of the religious roots of the practice, and who consider yoga only a form of fitness training. On the other hand, we have practitioners who fully believe in the associated Eastern religious tenets (be they Buddhist or Veda or something else in origin). Neither of these groups qualifies as spiritual somethingists (the first group does not even qualify as participating in a spiritual practice, while the second qualifies as traditionally religious). Instead, we find the spiritual somethingists in the big group in the middle. In this group, the subjects appreciate the transmundane character of yoga while their theoretical understanding is vague and unarticulated. They feel there is more to it than fitness training but are not willing to accept the traditional religious interpretation either (or they might be old religion somethingists as well and accept some vague version of the traditional picture).

To get a good understanding of New Spirituality Somethingism, it will be illuminating to take a closer look on a version not as entangled with traditional religion as yoga. Therefore, in what follows we will consider spirituality centred on feelings of interconnectedness with nature. Such spirituality, common in most countries in the West, is especially prevalent in regions with a strong tradition of outdoor life, such as the Pacific North-West in North America (Bramadat 2022) or Scandinavia in Europe (Thurfjell et al. 2019). For Nones embracing this kind of spirituality, nature is not only the primary context for existential thinking and exploring spiritual matters. For these somethingists, nature is itself the object of spirituality; it is their TSB.

New Spirituality Somethingism comes in both a weak and a strong version. When it comes to nature spirituality, the weak sense seems to be the most prevalent. These people seek out the natural world to feel connected, to escape everyday life, and so on (i.e. to have transmundane experiences), but they do not believe that anything supernatural exists in nature. In a scholarly report on nature spirituality in Denmark, where it usually is conducted by taking solitary walks on the beach, it is concluded that:

> The beach is felt to have a transformative potential for the solitary walkers . . . in this setting, you can escape society – and your social self – and become one with another world. Almost unanimously, our interlocutors highlight the

wind and the sensation of being "blown through" (in Danish, *blæst igennom*) as an energizing and cleansing feeling. (Thurfjell et al. 2019: 202)

In its strong form, nature spirituality is about more than escaping everyday life and feeling connected to the natural world. It is about feeling connected to something larger, something transcendent existing in connection to and beyond the natural world. While nature spirituality might be considered animism in a broad sense, by treating nature as TSB, some followers of the strong version come close to animism in the traditional sense of regarding nature as inhabited by transcendent personal forces. Here follows a telling example from Sweden (where it is the forest rather than the beach which is of existential significance):

> Maybe it's when I'm out running, then I stop . . . it's become a bit of a habit . . . I stop. There is a particularly beautiful place in a small wooded area over there, and I stand there for a few minutes . . . Then it doesn't become this usual inner dialogue, it becomes a dialogue with "something". (Thurfjell 2020: 213)

This subject explicitly uses the word 'something' to refer to the transcendent in nature (perhaps a transcendence restricted to a specific wooded area?), which demonstrates how this new spirituality ties in with Somethingism. As several studies have shown, practitioners of nature spirituality often have difficulties putting words on what they believe or experience. Many reach for the old Christian vocabulary but feel that it is inadequate, and that it is more of an approximation than literally true when they say that the forest is 'almost holy' or 'a little sacred' (Thurfjell et al. 2019: 207; Bramadat 2022: 31). Some go completely apophatic and claim that putting nature experiences into words would 'tarnish' them (Thurfjell 2020: 222).

For present purposes, it is especially interesting to notice that the typical spiritual somethingists have other reasons than old religion somethingists for accepting a thin view. There is no reductive thinning of some traditional and somehow unacceptable view. Instead, practitioners of new kinds of spirituality turn to Somethingism because they feel that their words are inadequate when confronted with the transmundane. The resulting view is thereby 'thin due to insufficiency of language'.

Life Question Somethingism

Consider the big, existential life questions, like 'What is a human?', 'What is the meaning of life', or 'What happens when we die'? Traditional religious worldviews almost always have deep and satisfying answers to these questions (that is, if you find them believable). If you pose these questions to naturalistic worldviews, they tend to provide answers too, but perhaps seldom the answers we wish for. In fact, naturalistic answers often strike us as somewhat depressing as compared to their religious counterparts. For example, the answer 'our consciousness disappears, and our bodies decompose' is not a very uplifting answer to the question 'what happens when we die?', especially if we compare it to traditional Christian answers, like heaven or resurrection (arguably, it is better than some traditional religious answers like hell, but that is not the point here). Therefore, it should not be surprising that naturalistic answers to the life questions are among the aspects of a naturalistic worldview many Nones reject.

Life Question Somethingism is simply when Nones turn to Somethingism in order to have an answer to one or many life questions. Like in other forms of Somethingism, the central idea which is supposed to answer the question is the unspecific view that a TSB which is at least transmundane exists.

> **Life Question Somethingism**: The existence of a TSB, which is at least transmundane and described without much detail, is postulated to answer one or many life questions.

As an illustration, here follows a quote from a Swedish life question somethingist, focused on the meaning of life and the afterlife (note how this textbook somethingist explicitly demarcates against both naturalism and traditional religion):

> I have these typical moments when it feels like there is some meaning to it after all. I immediately start to think to myself that "you should not confuse this with the idea that there is an omnipotent power behind it all" ... I see people that obviously manage to be atheists and to think that when you are dead, you are dead ... I just cannot do that. I need to believe in a greater meaning, and also, as a matter of fact, in a life after this, in order to feel completely at ease. (Burén 2015: 198)

Life Question Somethingism can in principle be both weak and strong, but while a strong version always seems feasible, it depends on which life question we are considering if a weak version would be adequate. If the question is 'What happens when we die?', it is hard to see how a transmundane answer will be satisfying (on the assumption that we want an answer where we survive death). Except, of course, if we take extravagant transmundane views like simulation theory into account. On the other hand, if the question is 'What is the meaning of life?', there is nothing preventing us from giving an answer in terms of Weak Somethingism.

Regarding some life questions, Life Question Somethingism is often combined with Old Religion Somethingism. This is especially the case when it comes to questions about an afterlife. This means that when the Nones add details to the TSB, it is usually ideas taken from traditional religion. Many American and spiritual Nones believe in reincarnation. However, not many details remain from traditional Eastern accounts of reincarnation. For example, few believe in moksha or nirvana, as it is reincarnation itself which has become the sought-after afterlife (Mercandente 2014: 207–221). While some Nones might have replaced the traditional Eastern details with something else, many hold vague, home-made views about reincarnation (or, to be more specific, about the TSB which makes reincarnation possible), thereby placing themselves on the Somethingism spectrum.

The somethingist's answers to the life questions are thin due to neither reductive thinning nor insufficiency of language. The Nones seek answers to the life questions, and it seems to us that they do not actually prefer their answers to be vague, but that they settle for abstract and vague answers because they cannot find any concrete and detailed answers in which they can believe. They have adopted their thin views because they lack belief in any detailed propositions which would provide a concrete answer. The content of their views is thereby 'thin due to ignorance'.

In this section, we have developed an understanding of Somethingism as commitment to an existentially significant and life-enhancing TSB (truly significant being). We have distinguished between a weak transmundane and a strong transcendent type. Moving beyond Pure Somethingism, we presented three main varieties: Old Religion Somethingism, New Spirituality Somethingism, and Life Question Somethingism. In relation to these types, we also distinguished between three different reasons to turn to an abstract and vague view: due to thinning, due to insufficiency of language, and due to ignorance. In what follows, we embark from this understanding, and put our distinctions to use, in a discussion of the rational and existential feasibility of Somethingism. In the upcoming section we consider questions of epistemic rationality and whether Somethingism can satisfy the demands of reason. It is followed by Section 4, where we consider Somethingism's ability to guide our lives and actions, and whether it can be existentially significant.

3 The Rationality of Somethingism

After having given a philosophical account of Somethingism, we now turn to the question of whether Somethingism can meet the rational feasibility challenge (here repeated for ease of reference):

> *The Rational Feasibility Challenge* concerns evaluating worldviews by assessing their coherence, consistency, and justification. It primarily involves scrutinising the core commitments of worldviews and their adherence to

public evidence. Meeting the challenge means demonstrating that a certain worldview is coherent with the demands of reason.

We are addressing the epistemic rationality of Somethingism in three separate ways. In Section 3.1 we consider the rationality of adopting a view with thin content, emphasising the difference between generality and vagueness. Is it always rational to settle for a more general view since it has a higher probability of being true? In Section 3.2 we consider the possibility of giving an evidential argument for Somethingism, using natural theology and the teleological fine-tuning argument as our point of departure. In Section 3.3 we consider the epistemic rationality of Somethingism in relation to non-doxasticism, an important contemporary beliefless approach to religion.

3.1 The Rationality of Thinning

Somethingism's characteristic feature is its thin content. The ideal of choosing your own worldview is dominant among the Nones, and adopting a view with thin content is generally a conscious choice. We are aware of no somethingists who, like many adherents of traditional religion, claim they have a thin view because that is how they were raised or because it is the norm in their community (although arguably, this is actually the case in countries like Sweden). Assessing the epistemic rationality of adopting a thin view is therefore even more relevant than giving a corresponding treatment to a traditional view.

In the previous section, we distinguished between three reasons the Nones might have for preferring a thin view. First, we considered thinning due to unacceptability. In this process a subject moves from a traditional, detailed view she is having difficulties accepting towards the abstract and unarticulated, until she finds an acceptable more general proposition. Such a view, we said, is 'thin due to unacceptability'. The second reason we considered is when a None adopts a view which is 'thin due to insufficiency of language'. In this case, the None experiences her TSB as in some sense ineffable – at least in the sense that the words springing to mind have the wrong connotations. Finally, we considered cases where a None adopts a thin view because she fails to give a concrete answer to some important life question. This None does not actually prefer a thin view, but it is the best she can produce. This view is 'thin due to ignorance'.

Drawing on the familiar distinction between epistemic and pragmatic reasons for belief, it seems that thinning due to unacceptability can be done for both pragmatic and epistemic reasons. Thinning to produce a believable view is done for epistemic reasons, and thinning to make a view acceptable due to other concerns (like the avoidance of patriarchal language) is pragmatic. Likewise, the main difference between ignorant thinning and thinning due to insufficiency of language is that the former is done for epistemic reasons, and the latter for practical. Ignorance is clearly an epistemic problem, while it must be considered a practical problem when a subject's vocabulary fails to capture the relevant phenomena.

There seems to be no epistemically significant differences between the epistemic reasons for thinning due to unacceptability and the epistemic reasons for thinning due to ignorance. In both cases, the None involved is unable to believe in any detailed view and turns to a thinner view which she finds believable. Whether she started with a detailed view which she thinned down or whether she adopted the thin view because it was her best conceivable option matters little from an epistemic perspective. The primary reason for adopting a thin view is that belief in the relevant detailed alternatives seems unjustified to the subject. This suggests that thin views are standardly a second-best alternative, a kind of retreat position when a full-blown detailed view is epistemically unavailable. But what are the epistemic advantages of adopting a thin view, and are there any drawbacks a None considering such a retreat position needs to be aware of?

Thinning makes a view more general, and sometimes also more vague. Weak Pure Somethingism is both general and vague, while the strong version is only general. The notion of the transmundane might be intuitive, but it is extremely vague since the border between the mundane and transmundane is anything but well defined. By contrast, transcendency is not a vague notion since the border between the empirical world of science and whatever might lie beyond is well-defined (there are no half-empirical phenomena). The thin views of Qualified Somethingism are often both general and vague, since the added qualifications tend to be vague.

It is important to treat vagueness, which is philosophically problematic, separately from generality, which is epistemically advantageous. Vagueness is usually contrasted with ambiguity. While the latter can be dissolved through disambiguation, vagueness always comes with borderline cases which are impossible to dissolve without leaving natural language behind. Standard examples include descriptive terms like 'bald' or 'obese' (there is no exact limit of how fat you must be to be obese). Some examples of Qualified Somethingism like 'something, like a good force, exists' are both ambiguous and vague. 'Good' and 'force' are ambiguous and can have multiple meanings ('good' as in positive evaluation or axiologically 'good', 'force' can be read both literally and metaphorically), but even when their meanings are specified, the remaining terms are still vague. 'Good' is vague simply because there are moral borderline cases, while 'force' has been made consciously vague by the addition of the vagueness indicator 'like' (other vagueness indicators include 'kind of', 'sort of', and the suffix '-ish').

Vagueness has received much philosophical attention and is generally considered an obstacle for rational thought and philosophical investigation. Since vague terms lack a determined meaning, they threaten the principle of bivalence (i.e. the requirement that a proposition must be either true or false) which is fundamental for all reasoning and inquiry (Fine 2020: 6–8). If a term lacks fixed meaning, it will not be obvious when it is true or false. For example, it is not obvious whether the view 'something like a good force exists' is true or false in a scenario where a collective of superhuman agents intervene in human affairs and bring about results which are beneficial for some people but do so for their own inscrutable ends. The common advice in philosophy to avoid vagueness is something the Nones should take care to follow.

It has been noted by several scholars that many Nones make their views intentionally vague (Thurfjell 2020: 222). While these cases might constitute harmless attempts at thinning, vagueness can also be sought in a way which can only be described as epistemically irresponsible. Consider the following example. Peter wants to believe that the God of perfect being theism exists, but in his view, gratuitous suffering is conclusive evidence against the existence of a God who is both omnipotent and perfectly good. To solve the problem, Peter adds a vagueness indicator and adopts the vague view 'something sort of like God exists'. If Peter's only motivation is to avoid falsification, the move surely seems ad hoc and highly questionable. You cannot, in general, turn to vagueness whenever the evidence suggests that you are wrong. However, if, in the same circumstance Peter where to seek generality rather than vagueness, that would not be questionable, although the process of thinning would be almost identical.[22]

Unlike vagueness, generality is epistemically advantageous, because the more general and without details a claim is, the more likely it is to be true. As put by Roy Sorenson:

> Generality is obviously useful ... If uncertain about which channel is the weather channel, she can hedge by describing the channel as 'forty-something'. There is an inverse relationship between the contentfulness of a proposition and its probability: the more specific a claim, the less likely it is to be true. By gauging generality, we can make sensible trade-offs between truth and detail. (Sorenson 2022: 5)

---

[22] In Peter's case, an acceptable alternative would be 'an ultimate reality with personal aspects exists'.

Semi-Secular Worldviews and the Belief in Something Beyond 31

Given these considerations, it is easy to see how thinning of content can be epistemically fruitful. If we adopt as a principle to always prefer a more general view over a more detailed view, we maximise our chances of having a true view, and by rejecting any detailed claims which might turn out to be false, we minimise the probability of believing falsehoods. Let us call this the principle of generality:

> **Principle of Generality (PG)**: In order to maximise our chances of believing truth and minimise the probability of believing falsehoods, we should always prefer a more general view over a more detailed one.

One philosopher who has repeatedly argued that we should follow a principle like PG is Schellenberg (2009; 2013; 2019b). In his view, we should commit only to the most general of all religious claims, which he identifies with the proposition that a triply transcendent reality exists, a view identical with Pure Strong Somethingism. The truth of any detailed religious view entails the truth of Pure Strong Somethingism. For example, if God exists, then a triply transcendent reality exists, and the same is true if Dao exists, or if a Buddha nature exists, or if the pantheon of Old Norse or Ancient Egyptian mythology exists.

It seems obvious that Nones who move from traditional religion to Somethingism are moving in the right direction according to PG. The probability that the TSB of Somethingism will turn out to exist is much greater than the probability that some traditional religion has got it all right. There are simply many more possible scenarios in which the general claim 'a TSB exists' is true than scenarios in which a claim like 'the God of perfect-being theism exists' is true.

PG also suggests that we should prefer Pure Somethingism over any qualified version. The more content we add, the less likely it is that a claim turns out to be true. 'Something transcendent exists' is more probable than 'something, like a higher justice exists', and we should therefore prefer the former view and refrain from adding any details to it. Since everything which is transcendent is also transmundane, and since there is much which is only transmundane without being transcendent, it is obvious that Weak Somethingism is a more general view than Strong Somethingism. PG therefore insists that we choose Pure Weak Somethingism, as it is the view with the highest probability of being true. But is it rational to stick to PG in all circumstances, or are there other important epistemic principles the somethingist also needs to consider?

William James famously argued that we have two main epistemic duties, to know truths and to avoid believing falsehoods. He also noted that these two duties often collide with one another, and that when we prioritise one duty above the other, we end up with a very different set of beliefs than if we had prioritised otherwise:

> *We must know the truth*; and *we must avoid error*, – these are our first and great commandments as would-be knowers; but they are not two ways of stating an identical commandment, they are two separate laws. Although it may indeed happen that when we believe the truth *A*, we escape as an incidental consequence from believing the falsehood *B*, it hardly ever happens that by merely disbelieving *B* we necessarily believe *A*. We may in escaping *B* fall into believing other falsehoods, *C* or *D* . . . Believe truth! Shun error! – these, we seem are two materially different laws; and by choosing between them we may end by coloring differently our whole intellectual life. (James 2010: 16, italics in original)

Isaac Levi expressed the same idea by suggesting that there are several different, sometimes conflicting epistemic utilities we need to balance when acquiring beliefs. According to Levi, the two most important utilities are truth and information, which roughly correspond to James's two duties of shunning error and believing truth (Levi 1967: 75–76).

PG is a principle dedicated to avoiding falsehoods rather than believing as many truths as possible. As we move to greater generality to avoid error, our number of beliefs is constantly lowered. Just think of the difference between believing, on one hand, all the propositions of a traditional, Christian worldview, with its rich metaphysical teachings about a triune personal God, incarnated and heavily involved in bringing salvation to a humankind tarnished by sin, and, on the other, believing the one proposition 'a transmundane reality exists'. The pure weak somethingist has clearly done her best when it comes to avoiding falsehoods, but the resulting view boils down to one single belief. The traditional Christian, one the other hand, has thousands of beliefs, and while she is in much greater risk of being in error, she might also end up believing thousands of truths.

Does this mean that the pure weak somethingist who follows PG to the letter is in some sense irrational or at least epistemically blameworthy? Not necessarily. It is true that James argued against being overly cautious, since there could be many important truths one might miss by always making it a priority to avoid falsehoods. It is also true that an epistemic subject who always prioritises truth over information ends up in an unfeasible situation, believing only propositions like 'I think' and 'something exists' or 'something happens'. However, James (2010: 16) emphasised that there is no further epistemic principle by which the matter might be settled, and he suggested that which duty we prioritise might ultimately be a matter of personal temperament. Therefore, we cannot on epistemic grounds criticise the pure weak somethingist for doing anything wrong.

Once we realise that there are other epistemic utilities beside avoiding false beliefs, we will see that all other forms of Somethingism stand for other, less radical ways of striking a balance between them. The pure strong somethingist might lie close to the weak, but the proposition she believes is nonetheless much richer in information. In Qualified Somethingism, we see a true trade-off between information and truth, because here we find a clear attempt to say something substantial about TSB while at the same time keeping the view as general as possible.

3.2 Somethingism, Evidence, and Natural Theology

Natural theology is the subdiscipline of philosophy of religion dedicated to arguments concerning the existence of God.[23] Most of these arguments presuppose evidentialism,[24] the common epistemic view that a belief is rational insofar as it is properly based on the relevant evidence. In this section, we are considering what evidential support can be mustered in defence of Somethingism.

One popular form of argument in natural theology is the likelihood argument. It is a modest kind of argument, which does not try to tell us what to believe, but only which of several competing hypotheses that is best supported by some specific set of evidence. It rests on the likelihood principle, which has been described as follows by natural theologian Robin Collins:

> This principle can be stated as follows. Let h_1 and h_2 be two competing hypotheses. According to the Likelihood Principle, an observation e counts as evidence in favor of hypothesis h_1 over h_2 if the observation is more probable under h_1 than h_2. Put symbolically, e counts in favor of h_1 over h_2 if $P(e|h_1) > P(e|h_2)$, where $P(e|h_1)$ and $P(e|h_2)$ represent the *conditional probability* of e on h_1 and h_2, respectively. (Collins 2009: 205)

Conditional probability concerns the probability of some evidence on a hypothesis and is a straightforward way of conceiving the idea of evidential support. For example, if our observational evidence is that 'Simon is joyfully eating an ice cream', this is much more probable on the hypothesis that 'Simon likes ice cream' than on the hypothesis 'Simon hates ice cream'. A likelihood argument is comparative, and the standard procedure is to compare the conditional probability of the evidence on theism with the conditional probability of

---

[23] Natural theology is generally contrasted with revealed theology and set apart from the former in that it only uses reason and public evidence rather than any alleged revelation (for an introduction, see Taliaferro 2009).

[24] We concentrate on evidential arguments and leave a priori arguments for another occasion.

the evidence on naturalism. It would therefore be interesting to see what the result would be if we introduced Somethingism as a third option. However, as will be apparent as we continue, it seems that the main question is not really whether the evidence supports Somethingism better than theism, but whether the evidence supports Somethingism at all.

Among the many arguments of natural theology, one of the oldest, most famous, and widely discussed is the teleological argument, aka the argument from the orderliness of the universe to the existence of God. It is beyond the scope of this text to consider all arguments from natural theology, and we therefore offer a focused treatment of Somethingism and the teleological argument in order to make some general points.

Historical versions of the teleological argument usually concern the general order of the universe, like in Paley's famous watchmaker analogy. In contemporary natural theology however, a new version known as the fine-tuning argument has come to dominate. The fine-tuning argument rests on the remarkable discovery in astrophysics that the universe seems to be fine-tuned for the existence of life. Of all the possible values the parameters of the universe could have taken, only a ridiculously small fraction would give rise to a life-permitting universe. Yet, in our universe, each parameter has just the right value for life to be possible, which is known as the 'anthropic coincidences':

> A series of breakthroughs in physics and observational astronomy led to the development of the Big Bang model and the discovery that the Universe is highly structured, with precisely defined parameters such as age, mass, entropy (degree of disorder), curvature, temperature, density and rate of expansion ... The specificity of the Universe prompted theoretical exploration of how the Universe would have been if the values of its parameters had been different. This led to the discovery of numerous "anthropic coincidences" and supported the claim that the Universe is fine-tuned for life – that is, that the values of the parameters are such that, if they differed even slightly, life of any sort could not possibly have arisen in the Universe. (Manson 2003: 4)[25]

The argument from the 'anthropic coincidences' to the existence of God is straightforward, especially when put as a likelihood argument. The whole point with the 'anthropic coincidences' is that a life-permitting universe is extremely improbable given naturalistic presumptions. It is a remarkable coincidence in demand of an explanation. On theism, on the other hand, a life-permitting universe is only to be expected if God exists. To put it formally in Collins'

---

[25] For a more detailed presentation of the fine-tuning data, see Collins (2009: 211–222) and Swinburne (2004: 172–188).

terms, P (anthropic coincidences | theism) > P (anthropic coincidences | naturalism).

What should we say about the conditional probability of the anthropic coincidences on Somethingism? It might be worth noticing that any theory which can explain these coincidences, whether they invoke something transcendent or only 'natural' phenomena like a multiverse,[26] would most likely entail the truth of Somethingism in the most general (i.e. weak) sense, since it is hard to envision an explanation which would not be at least transmundane. In this sense the probability of the anthropic coincidences on Somethingism is, of course, very close to 1. But this is just the advantage of generality differently put.

It might be more interesting to consider Somethingism as an *explanation* of the 'anthropic coincidences'. Probability aside, what Collins and other proponents really argue for is that a designer hypothesis like theism offers a much better explanation of the fine-tuning data than does any purely naturalistic alternative. From this perspective, the generality of a 'thin' view suddenly becomes problematic. To see why, consider Oppy's argument against any attempt to explain the 'anthropic coincidences' by postulating a cosmic designer:

> Given only the hypothesis that there is an intelligent designer of a universe – and given no further assumptions about the preferences of that designer – it is not clear to me that there is very much that one can conclude about the kind of universe that the designer is likely to produce. (Oppy 2006: 207)[27]

Oppy argues that one cannot properly explain the 'anthropic coincidences' by postulating a cosmic designer without also specifying the aims and goals of this designer, because one's theory is then too general to explain anything. While we believe that Oppy is wrong in this instance – invoking a designer as an explanation includes postulating that the designer has the motives required for designing what is to be explained, this is not an ad hoc addition as Oppy seems to suggest – the general idea behind his objection is crucial for understanding why Somethingism often fails as an explanation.

The core of Oppy's objection is that it depends on the details if an explanation succeeds in raising the probability of that which is to be explained or not. It is devastating for any attempt to use Pure Weak Somethingism as an explanation, since it is a view void of details. Pure Weak Somethingism is actually a worse

---

[26] Multiverse theories are a common naturalistic response to the anthropic coincidences. The general idea is that while it is extremely improbable that any universe should have life-permitting parameters, it is not very improbable that at least one such universe exists if we assume the existence of a vast number of universes. See, for example, Greene (2011).

[27] For another version of this argument, see Sober (2003, pp. 38–39).

explanation than platitudes like 'it happened for a reason' or even 'it happened because it happened' which at least inform us that something has caused something to happen.

Pure Strong Somethingism does not seem to fare much better in relation to the teleological fine-tuning argument. Without any details concerning its nature, it is hard to see how the idea that a triply transcendent reality exists could explain the 'anthropic coincidences'. There is simply nothing in this idea that makes the existence of a life-permitting universe more probable.

Can any qualified version of Somethingism explain the 'anthropic coincidences'? That depends on whether they include any information about TSB which makes the fine-tuning more likely. 'Something, like a higher justice' certainly concerns life, but it does not seem like the kind of phenomenon which orders universes. 'Something like a good force' is more on the right track, since a good force is a more suitable candidate for ordering a universe. If the good force is personal, it might be a designer, and if not, it might be something like the ancient idea of logos as a world-ordering principle – and of course it can be more Christ-like and be both. However, since there might also be good forces which do not design universes, like Dao or Buddha fields, it seems that we once again have to agree with Oppy that there is not much we can say before we get clear on the details.

It is not the level of details itself which determine whether a view can serve as an explanation, but rather whether relevant information is included. Imagine that you find a corpse in the wilderness and try to explain why this person has died. In such a situation, 'something poisonous bit him' is a fully acceptable explanation (given that it fits the evidence) even though it lacks any details on the concrete nature of this 'something'. On the other hand, a full description of Amsterdam (or something else completely irrelevant) cannot serve as explanation of the dead person, even though it is maximally detailed.

While it is obvious that almost no actual version of Qualified Somethingism contains the information required to explain the 'anthropic coincidences', it seems entirely possible to construct a version of Qualified Somethingism which does. 'Something, like a cosmic designer, exists' or 'Something, like a multiverse, exists' are obvious examples (note that the first is a qualified version of Strong Somethingism and the latter of Weak Somethingism). An answer to the question of why the universe is life-permitting seems a perfectly viable form of Life Question Somethingism. We are aware of no surveys reporting that actual Nones are responding to the 'anthropic coincidences' in this way (Life Question Somethingism seems to be restricted in actuality to issues such as the meaning of life and the existence of an afterlife). However, it is the philosopher's task to point towards intellectually feasible versions of the ideas we consider. We therefore want to invite the Nones pondering the unlikeliness of a life-permitting universe to consider a variety of Life Question Somethingism which incorporates only the information required to provide a reasonable explanation for the 'anthropic coincidences'.

These results generalise to any evidential natural theological argument. Pure Weak Somethingism is too general to explain anything. We need a qualified version with enough information to explain the evidence on which the argument in question builds. Consider the Liebnizian cosmological argument for the existence of God, which relies on the intuition that everything needs an explanation.[28] A deity can explain the existence of the universe insofar as it has the right powers and the right intentions, as the God of classical theism is usually depicted as having. The bare claim that a transmundane TSB exists lacks any information an explanation needs. Likewise, the Leibnizian cosmological argument asks for an explanation of everything, and 'why does the universe exist?' is surely a textbook life question. We can therefore construct an acceptable version of Qualified Life Question Somethingism which answers this question with the view that 'something, like a creator-deity, exists'.

Strong Somethingism warrants special attention here. Unlike Weak Somethingism, the strong version offers some information about TSB, namely that it is metaphysically, axiologically, and soteriologically transcendent. While this information does not get it very far with respect to the teleological argument, there are other arguments in natural theology where the postulation of a triple transcendence seems relevant. We are especially thinking of the Thomistic cosmological argument according to which there must be a transcendent metaphysical ground for everything, and the moral argument, which claims that the existence of (objective) moral values is more probable on theism than on naturalism.[29] It seems obvious that the existence of a transcendent metaphysical ground would be more likely on the assumption that a metaphysical transcendent reality exists, than on the naturalistic assumption that no such reality exists. Likewise, fitting objective moral values within a naturalistic framework is notoriously difficult and there are no uncontroversially successful attempts. Therefore, it also seems that the existence of objective moral values is more probable on the assumption that an axiologically transcendent reality exists. In all, it must be concluded that the conditional

---

[28] Other important versions include the Thomistic, which claims that everything needs a metaphysical ground, and the *kalam* argument, which claims that an actual eternity is impossible and so everything needs a beginning (for an oversight, see Pruss 2009).

[29] For some contemporary versions of the Thomistic argument, see Siniscalchi (2018) or Pearce (2017) (though the letter refers to it as the argument from contingency). For contemporary versions of the moral argument, see Linville (2009) and Swinburne (2004).

probabilities of a metaphysical ground and objective moral values are higher on Strong Somethingism than on naturalism.

But what about Oppy's objection? Is the triple transcendency view really detailed enough to explain objective moral values or a ground of everything? First, it must be acknowledged that these are evidential arguments in a much looser sense than the fine-tuning argument. The 'anthropic coincidences' are hard facts, while the existence of a metaphysical ground or objective moral values are philosophical theses which must be supported by arguments of their own. Second, if you believe in objective moral values, and are puzzled by the fact that they exist, postulating axiological transcendency seems like, if not itself an explanation, then at least a step towards an explanation. The same holds for a metaphysical ground. If you believe that a metaphysical ground exists but cannot see how it could exist in a naturalistic universe (perhaps you have adopted the venerable Thomistic view that it must be a necessary being), learning that a metaphysical transcendency exists might clear things up.[30]

The upshot of this section is that natural theological reasoning does not seem to support Somethingism very well. While Weak Somethingism is coherent with any view which could be supported by natural theological reasoning, it is also too general to explain any evidence. Strong Somethingism seems to fare somewhat better, but its evidential support is far from robust. Best supported are the versions of Qualified Life Question Somethingism which are answers to life questions concerning the phenomena natural theologians try to explain, but they are only a small minority of all possible qualified versions, and as far as we know, they have few (if any) adherents. However, we strongly suggest that Nones who would prefer to have evidential support for their Somethingism take these forms of life question Somethingism seriously.

3.3 Non-Doxasticism and Somethingism

This far, we have assumed that the Nones *believe* that 'something exists'. Perhaps that presupposition is wrong. What if their primary epistemic attitude is not that of outright belief? In the philosophy of religion, non-doxasticism is becoming increasingly important, as it allows for a rational, realist religious stance even in situations where rational belief is unavailable. On a non-doxastic

---

[30] However, it might also be argued that to reach a truly satisfying explanation, we must qualify the view somewhat and say that our TSB is not just transcendent but ultimate. Its existence is thereby the most fundamental fact possible, and its value the highest possible, and since this TSB is both metaphysically and axiologically ultimate, it will follow that this is the ultimate ground of all objective value. If so, the view Schellenberg has defended under the name 'Ultimism' (i.e. that a metaphysically, axiologically, and soteriologically ultimate reality exists) is better supported by natural theological considerations than its weaker counterpart triple transcendency.

approach, belief is substituted by some epistemically weaker attitude, such as acceptance (Alston 1996), assumption (Howard-Snyder 2013), hope (Pojman 1986), or voluntary assent (Schellenberg 2005). In previous work, we have found that at least some semi-secular Nones relate to their worldviews through non-doxastic attitudes (Jonbäck & Palmqvist 2024; Palmqvist & Jonbäck 2023).

What does it matter whether a None hopes or accepts that a TSB exists rather than believes that it does? The main answer is that it matters greatly for attribution of rationality. The epistemic standards for rationality are more relaxed for non-doxastic attitudes as compared to the standards for belief. Rational belief that p requires that you have enough evidence to be justified in believing,[31] but non-doxasticism only requires desire and enough evidence to regard that p as an epistemic possibility. A bit more formally, the two necessary conditions are:

> **Conative condition**: S desires that p or considers the truth of p an overall good thing.
>
> **Epistemic condition**: S regards p as an epistemic possibility, and lacks outright belief that both p and $-p$.[32]

The conative condition simply states that the subject needs to have a positive attitude towards the truth of p. Non-doxastic attitudes are always voluntary, and without a positive attitude adopting one makes no sense. The epistemic condition states that the subject must regard p as possible and that non-doxastic attitudes are incompatible with both belief and disbelief.[33]

According to sociologists of religion like Mark Chaves (2010), we should not expect congruence in religion, either between thought and action or between different thoughts. Chaves exemplifies with a story (originally from Meyer Fortes) about the rainmaker who laughs at the idea of rain-dancing in the dry season:

> He once asked a rainmaker in a native culture he was studying to perform the rainmaking ceremony for him. The rainmaker refused, replying: "Don't be a fool, whoever makes a rain-making ceremony in the dry season?" (Chaves 2010: 1).

---

[31] At least on the evidentialist assumption that justification is a matter of having the right evidence. Obviously, there are many other theories about justification in contemporary epistemology, but regardless of which of these you prefer, you will find the requirements for non-doxastic attitudes less demanding.

[32] These conditions have been developed in a series of writings by Palmqvist (2019; 2021; 2023).

[33] Belief is here understood as outright belief, an all-or-nothing concept where a proposition either is part of the subject's worldview or not. The contrasting view where belief comes in degrees is rejected. This is mostly for theoretical reasons, to avoid having a messy middle-ground where belief and non-doxastic attitudes are mixed up.

Chaves takes this story to illustrate that the rainmaker (as an exemplary religious person) is irrational in terms of incoherence. Since the rainmaker claims to summon rain with his dance, the rainmaker should have been prepared to dance also (perhaps especially so) in the dry season. The rainmaker's refusal to dance when it would have been most natural to do so (from the anthropologist's perspective, at least) is taken to imply that he is irrational, and that he both believes that his dance produces rain and that it does not.

A non-doxastic perspective allows us to understand the rainmaker as a rational agent.[34] We can think of at least two possible interpretations. First, the rainmaker might only accept that his dance summons rain while doubting and being highly uncertain about it. Since non-doxastic attitudes are weak grounds for action, perhaps the rainmaker only regards rain-dancing as justified when the wet season is drawing near, and rain is coming anyway? Second, while lacking belief, the rainmaker might fear that there will be no rain season if he does not dance to make it happen, and dance for precautionary reasons.

Both these interpretations are rational reconstructions of what might be going on in the mind of the rainmaker. In all cases where a non-doxastic interpretation according to which the subject is rational is readily available, it is to be preferred over a contrasting interpretation according to which the subject is an irrational believer. This is simply a matter of following the principle of charity (Palmqvist & Jonbäck 2023: 595). We believe that much apparent religious 'incongruence' can be dissolved this way.

Like Somethingism, non-doxasticism represents a way in which a subject who lacks traditional religious belief can have a rationally acceptable religious life. While Somethingism is characterised by 'thinning' of content, a move towards a general view, non-doxasticism is characterised by 'thinning' of attitude, a move from belief to non-doxastic attitudes.

Given the requirements of non-doxasticism, it seems obvious that a None who adheres to Somethingism could also adopt a non-doxastic attitude towards the existence of a transmundane or transcendent TSB. It is hard to imagine a None embracing Somethingism without desiring its truth or judging it an overall good thing – such a None would presumably adopt naturalism instead. Also, the whole reason with 'thinning' the content is to arrive at an acceptable view, and it is hard to see how a view which is not an epistemic possibility could

---

[34] Obviously, there are also interpretations available on which the rainmaker is rational which do not invoke non-doxasticism. Perhaps the rainmaker refuses to dance in the dry season because he respects the cycle of seasons and tries to live in harmony with nature?

ever be acceptable (which suggests that we never thin exclusively for pragmatic reasons).

But does a None who has already adopted the 'thin' content of Somethingism really need to 'thin' her epistemic attitude as well? If you have already moved from, say, Evangelical Christianity to Somethingism, you have presumably done away with all the hurdles, removing any hard-to-believe details. A traditional religious worldview contains many elements which might be hard to believe, especially if it is interpreted literally, but if the view is 'thinned' down to pure Somethingism, what obstacles for belief can remain and what need can there be for adopting non-doxasticism? In general, a somethingist seems to have no need for non-doxasticism.

However, there are some major exceptions. We can see at least two kinds of cases where it would be reasonable for a None to combine Somethingism and non-doxasticism. The first is cases where the subject, even though she does not believe that naturalism is true, takes it to be probable enough to block outright belief in anything transcendent. In this situation, she has two options. She can either rest content with Weak Somethingism, which does not come with any transcendent claims, or she can non-doxastically adopt Strong Somethingism, because even though belief in the transcendent is out of the question, it still represents a desirable epistemic possibility.

The other scenario is when a None attempts to advance from pure Somethingism to a qualified version. In such a situation it might be the case that she finds no qualified view believable. While she feels confident enough to proclaim that she believes in 'something', she does not really believe in a higher power or some benevolent force in nature or something like that. In this scenario, it is important to see that the None does not necessarily disbelieve the qualified views she cannot believe. They might well represent desirable epistemic possibilities she can choose to accept non-doxastically.

An objector might grant that many somethingists could benefit from adopting non-doxasticism, but turn the tables and ask whether it is not the case that non-doxasticism makes Somethingism superflous? If you already are a non-doxastic Christian, Buddhist, or neo-pagan, it seems that your position is already rationally acceptable and that there is no need to 'thin' the content. How can this challenge be met?

First of all, there are presumably Nones who have reasons to believe that 'something' exists in a way where it would not make much sense to 'thin' the attitude. Imagine, for example, a None having a strong religious experience. She is unwilling to use traditional religious language to describe her experience, but afterwards she strongly believes that there is 'something more, like a life-force', beyond the world of our senses. Or imagine a philosophically inclined None who becomes convinced by the fine-tuning argument that there is a cosmic designer but who rejects all traditional accounts of gods and deities. This None believes that 'something like a cosmic designer exists', and it would make no sense for her to adopt a weaker epistemic attitude.

However, while Somethingism cannot always be substituted by non-doxasticism or vice versa, in many instances it would be possible for a None to handle an unbelievable religious claim either through thinning of content or attitude. In other words, most Nones have a choice between Somethingism and non-doxasticism (or at least they would have if they were philosophically informed about possible ways forward). It therefore seems appropriate to ask which of the two approaches a None should prefer.

We are doubtful whether Somethingism or non-doxasticism can be said to be superior on epistemic grounds alone. While it certainly seems reasonable to suggest that one should always prefer to *believe* truths, we have also seen that the generality of Somethingism makes it problematic from other perspectives. While compatible with almost all evidence, it explains very little, and it represents an extreme position when it comes to balancing information and truth. Non-doxasticism, on the other hand, allows its subjects to have as detailed a view as possible, but at the cost of eschewing belief in favour of weaker attitudes. When it comes to explanation, it seems that the necessary details are present, but any non-doxastic explanation will be highly hypothetical since it does not warrant belief.

However, apart from epistemic rationality, there are also practical matters of religious feasibility to consider. This is the topic of the next section. While it concerns the religious feasibility of Somethingism, we suggest that the reader keep non-doxasticism in mind as well. When we familiarise ourselves with the problems Somethingism encounters in this regard because of its generality, it is important to remember that there are other detailed approaches than traditional belief-based religion.

4 Living with Somethingism

A religious worldview usually has a massive impact on the lives of its adherents. Even if false, it comes with several benefits, and if true, it will provide goods far beyond what is achievable through any other means. As we saw in Section 1, both Nagel and Kitcher considered whether Naturalism could meet a similar function of providing hope and meaning, and of bringing the individual into a relationship with the deepest structure of the universe. Inspired by Nagel and Kitcher, we presented this as the existential challenge for worldviews (here repeated for ease of reference):

> *The Existential Feasibility Challenge* concerns the evaluation of a worldview's capacity to guide our lives, both in our day-to-day affairs and on the grand scale, towards alignment with the deepest levels of existence. It also concerns assessing its resources for coping with hardship and existential issues such as meaning and purpose.

What can we say about this challenge in relation to Somethingism? What kind of role can Somethingism play in the life of the Nones? Is it possible for Somethingism to play the same kind of significant role as traditional religion usually plays? If not, what kind of role should we expect instead?

In the upcoming Section 4.1 we address the fundamental issue of whether Somethingism contains enough information to allow for the None to interact with her TSB. Like in previous publications by Palmqvist (2019; 2022), we call this the alignment problem. In Section 4.2 we address the further question of how rich or substantial a religious-like life based on Somethingism can be. In Section 4.3 we consider what resources Somethingism contains to help the Nones deal with existential issues, like the problem of evil.

4.1 The Alignment Problem

The alignment problem concerns the None's ability to interact with her TSB. While the None's view is general and lacks details, reality itself is not without its details, and detailed conceptions are required to interact properly with it. We therefore have reasons to ask: if a None's particular version of Somethingism turns out to be true, does the view contain enough information to allow the None to interact with her TSB? We begin by considering the matter in relation to Pure Strong Somethingism, since this issue ties in with an existing debate between Schellenberg on one hand, and Andrew Dole and Palmqvist on the other. We later expand the discussion to cover other forms of Somethingism.

As earlier mentioned, Schellenberg has on numerous occasions defended the view that there exists a triply transcendent reality, which we call Pure Strong Somethingism.[35] In a critical discussion on Schellenberg's view, Dole (2013: 236–240) has pointed out that Pure Strong Somethingism is too general an outlook since it does not contain sufficient soteriological information. Even if Pure Strong Somethingism is true, and we truly believe that it is, we will have no idea of how to receive the greatest human good it offers (as soteriological transcendency). The greatest human good will be unavailable to us since we lack the needed, detailed information on how to receive it.[36] For example,

---

[35] To be more correct, he has defended non-doxastic faith in such a view (Schellenberg 2019b), just like he earlier defended non-doxastic faith in Ultimism (Schellenberg 2009; 2013).

[36] Except, of course, in a scenario where the greatest human good is distributed freely, 'by grace alone' and in no way requiring human action.

according to certain forms of Evangelical Christianity, salvation is only available for those who are 'born again'. Let us consider a scenario where this view is true. Here, the None who believes in Pure Strong Somethingism will believe the truth, namely that something triply transcendent exists, but she will have no idea that the triply transcendent is God or that she needs to be 'born again' to receive the greatest good (here: Christian salvation).

Palmqvist (2019; 2022) has developed the objection into the alignment problem. The notion of alignment he employs is broader than Dole's concept of soteriological information, and concerns the subject's overall ability to interact with transcendent reality:

> I understand alignment as [the subject] having a cognitive content which corresponds to reality, in combination with being guided in action by this content. Both components are needed for full alignment: if you act in alignment with reality but fail to have the proper cognitive attitude, you are poorly aligned – Don Quixote fighting windmills he believes to be giants is an example of this. If you have the right content without acting properly, you are also poorly aligned – imagine someone who [truly] believes that he sees a wall but acts as if it is not there and tries to walk right through it. (Palmqvist 2022: 98)

To be properly aligned, a subject must have the right cognitive content and act upon it. While it might have been more straightforward to formulate this as having true beliefs and acting upon them, this notion of alignment is compatible with non-doxasticism as well. Whether you believe or merely accept or hope that p is not significant.

Just like Dole's objection, the alignment problem was originally formulated in a critical discussion on what we call Pure Strong Somethingism. Its main point is that in a scenario where a triply transcendent reality exists, like a pantheon of gods, a life-force or a buddha-field, a subject adhering to Pure Strong Somethingism will truly believe (or have a positive non-doxastic attitude to) the general truth that 'a triply transcendent reality exists' but she will not be aligned to this reality. She will lack the cognitive content required for successful interaction with transcendent reality, since she will lack any ideas concerning its nature.

Consider an illustrative analogy. A force field separates one end of a room from the other. One end of the room is completely dark, the other is lit up. A person in the bright part can interact with objects and persons in the dark part through the field, but due to some mysterious property of the field, it is not possible to explore the dark by using the tactile sense. This means that one must have sufficient information concerning what is in the dark before attempting to interact with it. Otherwise the force field does not let you through.

Sally is situated in the bright side of the room. She knows that there is 'something' in the darkness, on the other side of the force field, which holds great value to her. That is all she knows. Obviously, she wishes to interact with 'something' to be able to access its great value. However, her true information is so general that it is useless. She cannot interact with the object in the dark unless she learns more details.

It might be suggested that Sally could have more information than we assume, because should she not be able to infer something useful from the fact that the object holds great value to her? Unfortunately, this is not the case, since the class of objects which can be said to have 'great value' to Sally is nearly endless. Does great value mean great personal value for her? In such a case, the dark may contain an important person, like her husband, or an important object, like her beloved scrapbook collection. Does it mean great practical value? If so, the dark part of the room could contain Sally's car. Could great value simply mean monetary value? In such case, it could be jewels, or perhaps just a bag full of cash sitting in the dark. And so on. Knowing that 'something' has great value is clearly not enough.

Would it be enough to know what *kind* of value the object has? While it could be argued that such knowledge would bring Sally one step closer to alignment, interaction would still be practically impossible since each value-category contains vastly different things: consider the great difference between interacting with one's spouse and a scrapbook.

The analogy is obvious: the object in the dark part of the room represents transcendent reality, and without having detailed information about it, a subject trying to interact with it will lack the means to do so properly because she lacks any detailed information about its nature.[37] Put a bit more formally, the alignment problem can be shaped into the following deductive argument:

$P1_{PSS}$: To interact with transcendent reality (if there is one), a subject must have detailed information concerning its nature.

$P2_{PSS}$: A subject adhering to Pure Strong Somethingism will lack any detailed information concerning the nature of transcendent reality.

C_{PSS}: A subject adhering to Pure Strong Somethingism cannot interact with transcendent reality (if there is one).

The first premise follows from our previous considerations, and the second from the definition of pure Strong Somethingism. The argument therefore seems to be both valid and sound.

---

[37] Of course, if transcendent reality is personal, like God, it might try to interact with the None (as Sally's husband might try in the example), but that is beside the point, since the None's own cognitive states will have no impact on this kind of interaction.

What are the consequences of this argument for other forms of Somethingism? Let us begin with Pure Weak Somethingism. The difference between pure Weak Somethingism and Pure Strong Somethingism is that the TSB of the weak version is transmundane rather than transcendent. At first glance, this might seem like a significant advantage. After all, a transmundane TSB exists in the world of our senses and not in a transcendent realm beyond experience. However, this apparent advantage is of little importance, since pure Weak Somethingism says nothing at all about the nature of TSB. To put it bluntly, the None will have no idea what object in the universe she is supposed to interact *with*.

Moving back to the illustrating analogy, the pure weak somethingist is in a version of the scenario where the room is fully lit and full of billions of objects. The problem is that while Sally knows that one of these objects holds great value, she has no idea which it is. Her knowledge is practically useless since it does not in any way tell her which object to interact with. Reshaping the deductive argument for Pure Weak Somethingism, we get:

$P1_{PWS}$: To interact with a TSB (if there is one), a subject needs to have detailed information concerning its nature.

$P2_{PWS}$: A subject adhering to pure Weak Somethingism will lack any detailed information concerning the nature of any TSB there might be.

C_{PWS}: A subject adhering to pure Weak Somethingism cannot interact with any TSB.

In other words, the lack of detailed information is as devastating for Pure Weak Somethingism as it is for Pure Strong Somethingism.

It seems obvious that qualified versions of Somethingism must fare better with regards to the alignment problem, since they are characterised by having the kind of detailed information the pure versions are lacking. It is, however, important to see that the qualified version needs to contain the right kind of additional details to have the ability to escape the problem. 'I believe in something, something fundamentally good which everything is part of' is still too general and vague to allow for alignment. What is required is information on the nature of TSB (be it transcendent or transmundane) which is specific enough to allow for interaction. As a minimum, Qualified Strong Somethingism needs to specify the nature of the transcendent to the degree that it becomes possible to act on the information. The None needs to know if TSB is approachable by means of prayer, meditation, ritual sacrifice, heightened awareness in everyday life, long-distance running, emotional devotion, or whatever the right way of interacting with the divine might be. By contrast, Qualified Weak Somethingism only needs to direct us towards the right object.

Qualified Old Religion Somethingism (which always builds on Strong Somethingism) seems well-equipped in this regard, since its TSB is a generalised version of the TSB of traditional religion. As long as it posits the same kind of transcendent reality as the traditional religion it builds upon, and the same kind of interaction, the None adhering to it should be properly aligned with its TSB. For example, say that Christianity is the true religion and that a None believes 'Something like a good personal force exists'. This None will presumably have the details sufficiently right to be able to interact with God.

However, it is important to note that it is not guaranteed that a None who is sufficiently aligned to interact is also sufficiently aligned to receive the greatest human good. This depends entirely on how right you must be to be properly aligned from a soteriological perspective. In the first example in this section, we assumed that Evangelical Christianity was the true religion and that one had to be 'born again' to receive salvation. On this picture, the None who believes in a good personal force will not be in possession of the relevant details. On the other hand, suppose that the Evangelical requirement is too strict, and that it is enough to be in a personal relationship with God. In this scenario, it seems fully possible that a None who believes in a good personal force and acts on this belief will be able to enter the right kind of saving relationship with God. Two points are important here. First, alignment seems to come in degrees, and a None's level of alignment might be sufficient for interaction while not being sufficient from a soteriological perspective. Second, what level of alignment that is required for interaction and for soteriological purposes depends entirely on the nature of TSB.

Insofar as Live Question Somethingism is based on Strong Somethingism, we do not think there are any relevant differences as compared to Old Religion Somethingism. It might, however, be worth pointing out that in standard cases, the interaction it can lead to will be limited to the aspects of the TSB which concerns its life question. For example, it will only be soteriologically relevant if the life question is about salvation. Live Question Somethingism based on Weak Somethingism will escape the alignment problem when its details allow us to identify its TSB.

To what extent New Spirituality Somethingism can avoid the alignment problem is a trickier issue. We have associated New Spirituality Somethingism with thinning due to insufficiency of language. This kind of thinning is more likely than the others to lead to vagueness. When language is inadequate, adding a vagueness-indicator is often your best shot at getting something through: 'When I do yoga, it *kind of* feels like a force moves through me' or 'The forest seems *almost a little* holy'. If the None really finds all words inadequate to describe the general area of her TSB, it seems reasonable to suggest that everything she says about it will be in some sense vague.

Vagueness is simply what you get when you attempt to say anything at all when language is insufficient. As mentioned in the previous section, vagueness is philosophically problematic since it is unclear how a vague statement relates to reality, that is, what its truth-conditions are. If alignment is a matter of having true, detailed information, it seems obvious that a None with a vague view will be cognitively less well-aligned than a None with well-defined information. If the view is sufficiently vague, it will even be impossible for an independent observer who knows the nature of TSB to determine whether the None is cognitively aligned or not.

However, when it comes to New Spirituality Somethingism, it is often the case that the None takes part in a spiritual practice, like yoga or long walks in nature, and that the inadequacy of language enters the picture first when the None tries to describe her experiences. It seems reasonable to suppose that such a None is aligned through action first-most, and through cognitive content only in a secondary manner. If such alignment is possible, perhaps the vagueness of their language need not prevent the Nones from aligning with TSB. However, this alignment will be less complete than one which builds on both cognitive content and action.

To summarise this section, it seems that pure versions of Somethingism cannot accommodate for the alignment problem, and that the more qualified a version of Somethingism the None adheres to, the better are her chances for alignment with TSB (if TSB exists and is a true TSB etc.). Also, vagueness is to be avoided because the vaguer a view gets, the less clear it is what is required for alignment to be possible.

4.2 Can Somethingism Play the Role of Religion?

The alignment problem concerns the Nones' ability to interact with TSB, to receive the benefits of being aligned with transmundane or transcendent reality. While we should certainly take the problem seriously, it is only relevant in a scenario where Somethingism is true. There are other practical concerns where the eventual truth of Somethingism is largely irrelevant (but, of course, the None herself must still believe or non-doxastically accept its truth). One such issue is discussed in the next section, which assesses Somethingism's resources to cope with existential problems. This section concerns another, namely the possibility for Somethingism to play a religion-like role in the

Nones' life. As in the previous section, we will begin by considering the matter in relation to pure Strong Somethingism, and then explore the consequences for the other types.

According to Schellenberg (2009: ch. 2), Pure Strong Somethingism is compatible with 'a clear and substantial religiousness' (Schellenberg 2009: 17). While Schellenberg's writings on the topic are extensive, we are going to focus on three suggestions concerning the possibility of conducting religious investigation, of taking moral action, and of leading a spiritual life.

Schellenberg suggests that the religious life of Pure Strong Somethingism will be characterised by religious investigation, in an attempt to fill out the details of this abstract view. This seems unobjectionable from our present perspective. Many Nones are religious seekers or explorers, and religious investigation is already an important part of their life. Furthermore, all the kinds of thinning of content we have considered depend on a lack of acceptable religious claims (a lack that might be due to epistemic reasons, pragmatic reasons, or insufficiency of language). Nobody, it seems, adopts Somethingism without first rejecting more detailed claims, and it therefore seems reasonable that a somethingist would be interested in adding new details to her view, if such details were available. We therefore find no reason to reject Schellenberg's suggestion. However, it is also clear that something more than religious investigation is needed if the None is to have a life akin to that of a religious believer. After all, a life might be centred on religious investigation and yet not be a religious life, like the life of an atheist religious scholar.

These considerations point to the conclusion that Pure Somethingism will be a rare position, held only by those who, after prolonged investigation, cannot accept any but the most general view. Even for those, it will only be a temporary position in principle, to be held until new acceptable detailed claims are discovered. As we shall see in what follows, there are also other, more theoretical reasons for thinking that Pure Strong Somethingism is actually a rare position.

Moral action is undoubtedly a vital part of a religious life. According to Schellenberg, holding the view that axiological transcendency exists in itself enables the subject to act morally, especially when it comes to 'risk-taking on behalf of the good'. His general idea is that if we (doxastically or not) accept the idea that an axiological transcendency exists, we will, so to speak, be backed up by the deepest layers of reality when we attempt to take moral action (Schellenberg 2009: 40–44). In a previous publication, we found reasons to reject Schellenberg's claim about risk-taking on behalf of the good as being overly Christian (Palmqvist 2022: 107–108). Here, we are instead going to consider the wider possibility of basing *any* moral action on Pure Strong Somethingism.

An adherent of Pure Strong Somethingism will lack any detailed information about the axiologically transcendent. Could she at the same time have enough detailed cognitive content to take moral action? We find such a suggestion incoherent. Having moral beliefs which are so specific that they enable taking moral action seems incompatible with Pure Strong Somethingism. If there is an axiologically transcendent reality, moral beliefs will depend on the axiologically transcendent for their truth, since an axiological transcendency will be the ground of every value. If you have a belief about something morally good, you must also have some idea, however vague, about the axiologically transcendent. If you claim to have moral beliefs but no detailed beliefs about the axiologically transcendent, you have failed to realise this connection, and your view on the axiologically transcendent is actually more detailed than you suppose.

The point that it is impossible to have moral beliefs while claiming to be ignorant about the axiologically transcendent is important.[38] It suggests that moral beliefs in combination with Strong Somethingism is in fact a form of qualified Strong Somethingism, and that pure Strong Somethingism requires you to be a moral agnostic as well as a religious agnostic. Of course, pure Strong Somethingism is also compatible with non-realist views on our actual moral practices. You might, for example, believe that our current morality is based on social convention or that it is a useful fiction, and that the true morality is as unknown as the true view on the axiological transcendency itself. Pure Strong Somethingism is also incompatible with nihilism since there can be no axiological transcendency in a world without values.

These conclusions strongly indicate that pure Strong Somethingism is a far less widespread view than we might have anticipated (and especially so if we also take into account that it must be understood as a temporary position). If having moral beliefs is in fact a way of qualifying Somethingism, it seems that most instances of Strong Somethingism will be qualified rather than pure (according to our taxonomy, they will be either Old Religion Somethingism or Life Question Somethingism, depending on whether the moral beliefs come from a religious heritage or whether they are an answer to a life question like 'how should I treat others?'). However, its theoretical clarity still makes pure Strong Somethingism a philosophically interesting position, and a natural centre of this discussion.

---

[38] This point is overlooked in the discussion on Schellenberg's view, and contrary to Schellenberg's own claims.

Now, let us consider the possibility of basing a spiritual life on Pure Strong Somethingism. In *Evolutionary Religion* Schellenberg (2013) offers an interesting thought experiment. Challenging the view that religious details are essential for having a religious attitude towards life, he considers a scenario where religion is *born* without details. It is centred on Genna, a human-like alien on a distant planet who, as the first member of her species, has a religious awakening. On this alien world, the first religion to appear is something very much like pure Strong Somethingism (or so claims Schellenberg):

> But then one of their number (let's call her Genna) has a profound experience. Unable to sleep and standing outside her tent flap, gazing at a spider's web,[39] she suddenly has a sense of possibilities greater than ever seen or imagined, a prolonged and astonishingly rich experience in which she seems plunged into something that comes from every direction and yet from none, further away than the mountains hunched over the valley and yet closer to her own breath and quivering with the spider's web. Something that fills everything with a light at once inviting and frightening. Something that with its terror and with its joy breaks up all the categories by which she had perceived the world into kindling for the fire and yet leaves her feeling utterly complete and whole … None of the particular conceptions she is able to spin from her great imagination is satisfying … The best she can do is to push her thinking in the opposite direction to take facets of her everyday experience, extend them as far as possible, and then imagining something beyond even that. So when swimming to the bottom of a tidal pool, she imagines a pool with no bottom; when gazing at the sheltering mountains she imagines a mountain that remains perpetually on the horizon, no matter how far she walks … In time, some of Genna's friends and acquaintances undertake their own experiments with Genna's idea, making it their own, and beginning to experience the world in a different light. (Schellenberg 2013: 87–89)

Genna's spirituality is based on a religious experience, which might be taken to indicate that her view is true. Schellenberg himself, however, does not take religious experience to indicate truth but only epistemic possibility (a view we endorse; see Palmqvist 2019: 568–571).[40] That Genna's spirituality is based on experience might also be taken to indicate that such experience would be necessary for this kind of spirituality. That is not what Schellenberg has in mind, which is illustrated by the fact that Genna is able to spread her view to other aliens who have not undergone the same kind of experience.

---

[39] Presumably, Schellenberg here refers to a spider-like creature native to Genna's world, as it would be extremely unlikely that actual spiders (with the same DNA and evolutionary history as the spiders of Earth) would evolve on more than one world, and it would be even more unlikely to find spiders from Earth on Genna's world.

[40] Schellenberg envisions Genna as a religious non-doxasticist. For clarity, we have left that part of her story out of the discussion.

Curiously, the kind of spirituality which emerges on this alien world seems familiar from the literature on the Nones. Just like the Nones of the New Spirituality variety, Genna's refusal to adopt a detailed view is based on insufficiency of language. The fact that her experiences seem to defy all her previous conceptions is the prime reason she keeps the view general. While this corresponds well to our New Spirituality Somethingism, it is somewhat unusual for Schellenberg who generally argues for thinning based on epistemic reasons. Neither does Schellenberg seem to notice that this makes Genna's view vague, and that she actually seems to lack the concept of a triply transcendent reality on which pure Strong Somethingism is based. Given our taxonomy, it seems highly questionable whether a person in Genna's place would really adhere to Pure Strong Somethingism, since she is lacking its distinct cognitive content.

In fact, it seems questionable to suggest that Genna's view is really without details. Her spirituality clearly seems connected to her experience of nature. Not only to the spider's web, which gives rise to her first experience, but also to the mountains and the tidal pool. Nature is not only the medium she experiences transcendent reality through, it is also what she uses to reach out for the transcendent, in thought and action. In short, Genna seems to practice something very much like the nature-centred Somethingism we find in our real world, and such spirituality is not without details. Since she relates to transcendent reality through nature, and not through the abstract idea of a triple transcendency, it seems natural to view Genna as an adherent of qualified New Spirituality Strong Somethingism of the nature-centred variety, and not as an adherent of pure Strong Somethingism.

The only spirituality based on pure Strong Somethingism we can imagine is meditation upon the idea of a triply transcendent reality. We are doubtful that such meditation without details would be a very meaningful activity. It seems much impoverished compared to what Genna is up to, and it cannot involve connecting the idea of a triply transcendent reality with the world as we experience it. Any attempt to do so would mean crossing the line into qualified Somethingism. This is the main point we wish to make in relation to the story of Genna.

To sum up the discussion, it seems that Schellenberg is right in claiming that a religious life based on Pure Strong Somethingism can contain religious investigation, but we reject the claims that it can include moral action or any substantial form of spirituality. In these areas, details are needed. It therefore seems inadequate as a ground for religious life – something more than religious investigation is clearly needed. Qualified versions of Somethingism seem much better candidates for the None who wants a life akin to that of traditional religion.

To complete the picture, we briefly want to address Pure Weak Somethingism. Since it only claims that a transmundane TSB exists somewhere in our universe, but refuses to say anything about it, we cannot see how this view can allow for any of the aspects of a religious-like life we have considered, except religious investigation. Clearly, it is a poor choice for any None who seeks to lead a life akin to that of traditional religion.

At this point, it might be worth asking how relevant this discussion is to the Nones. Do the Nones really want to live a life akin to the religious life of traditional religion? Or are most Nones happy with living a mostly secular life? Obviously, this is an empirical question, but we still want to offer some considerations we find relevant. First, many Nones are seekers of one form or other (Mercadante 2014: 53–57). This seems to suggest that these Nones are looking for something other than a secular life. Therefore, it seems reasonable that these Nones would be interested in the possibility of living a religious-like life based on what they already got. Second, we have seen that the different kinds of thinning by which the Nones reach Somethingism are based on different kinds of problems, epistemic or otherwise, which prevents them from adopting traditional religion. This also seems to suggest that the Nones would be interested in knowing how much of a religious life can be 'salvaged' on Somethingism. For these Nones, at least, we strongly suggest adopting qualified versions of Somethingism rather than the pure forms.

Before moving on, we also want to address the material side of religion. Dole (2013: 241–244) has criticised pure Strong Somethingism, in its Schellenbergian form, for not being religiously adequate. He presses the point that religions typically have a rich material culture, including things such as liturgy, architecture, symbols, rituals, holy scripture, and so on, which standardly builds on the details of a religious outlook. Dole finds it hard to envision how an abstract and general view could ever generate something similar.

While Dole certainly has a point, we think he overemphasises the need for details. Envision a gothic cathedral. Undeniably, in many places – like its windows, altar pieces, paintings, and statues – we find artistic representations of the detailed stories of Christian tradition (most notably the suffering of Christ). However, the central theme of the gothic cathedral is that of connecting our earthly existence with the heavens towards which it reaches, or to make it even less specifically Christian, of humanity reaching for the transcendent. Presumably, the idea that there is a soteriologically and axiologically transcendent reality is all we need to make sense of this great theme. Of course, that is not meant to deny that if we add some details to our conception of transcendent reality, like the idea that it is somehow personal and worthy of our prayer, this will only add to the impact of the cathedral. Neither do we wish to deny that a cathedral full of Christian imagery is in some sense superior to one void of imagery. We only want to stress the point that powerful religious architecture is possible on an abstract and overly Christian view.[41]

Since our space is limited, we leave it to the reader to figure out how these considerations concerning architecture apply to other parts of the material culture of religion. The point we wish to make is that developing a material culture based on general ideas in no way seems impossible. However, since it seems reasonable to suggest that the Nones interested in developing something corresponding to the material side of religion will also be the ones who desire a religious-like life, we are doubtful that the arguably few Nones who stick with Pure Strong Somethingism would be much interested in this possibility. Since adding details only makes it easier and perhaps also more meaningful to develop a material culture, we envisage that any development in this area will be in relation to Qualified Somethingism.

4.3 Somethingism, Existential Problems, and Existential Resources

In this section, we will continue setting the truth of Somethingism aside and consider whether or not embracing Somethingism can help a None dealing with existential issues. To keep the discussion manageable, we centre our attention on suffering and evil.

Problems of evil are often presented as theoretical challenges, typically focusing on Perfect Being Theism by questioning why a perfectly good, all-knowing, and almighty God permits evil or suffering that is not necessary for greater good(-s), so-called gratuitous suffering. The more precise argument can be formulated as follows:

(1) There are cases of gratuitous suffering.
(2) If God were to exist, there would be no cases of gratuitous suffering.

Therefore:

(3) God does not exist[42]

---

[41] The Muslim mosque is another example of how magnificent religious architecture can be based on simple but powerful ideas without much additional details. The architecture of the mosque symbolises the cosmos and its relation to the Creator, that is, it is built on the general but powerful idea of theism. Granted, some details, like the mihrab, build on specific Muslim ideas, but they are far less prevalent than in the cathedral. It is rather telling that the main change that was made in converting a cathedral like Hagia Sophia to a mosque was the covering up of Christian imagery. So while there is certainly something to Dole's objection – it is certainly harder to develop a material culture void of details – it seems exaggerated.

[42] Compare, for example, with Rowe (2006: 60).

The argument is valid and premise (2) can be supported when the following details about God are added:

(4) A perfectly good God does not want gratuitous suffering in the world.
(5) An all-powerful God can prevent all cases of gratuitous suffering.
(6) An all-knowing God is aware of all gratuitous suffering that exists.

Due to the lack of detail, Pure Weak Somethingism and Pure Strong Somethingism do not encounter such theoretical problems as the one outlined here. On the one hand, this might be considered as a great theoretical advantage of these general views. On the other hand, however, their generality also seems to imply a lack of the existential resources which more detailed descriptions of the transcendent contain. To get clear on what kind of resources we are considering, we return to Kitcher's existential criticism of naturalistic worldviews:

> For people whose lives are going badly, or that are in constant danger of going badly, religion can provide important forms of security, sometimes hope that the reversals of this life will be compensated in the next, and opportunities for mutual consolation. Part of this promise (the idea that the bad things that actually occur will somehow be redeemed) is not easily replicable in a secular framework. (Kitcher 2011: 34)

The idea here is that religion, and in particular traditional Christian religion building on Perfect Being Theism, comes with meaning and reasons for hope which Naturalism lacks. To see this, consider how an adherent of Perfect Being Theism might reject the argument just presented by turning it on its head, thereby using its resources to deny the existence of gratuitous suffering:

(not-3) God exists.
(2) If there is gratuitous suffering, then God does not exist.

Therefore:

(not-1) There are no cases of gratuitous suffering.

The suggestion is that God has a purpose with all suffering, and that seemingly gratuitous suffering in fact has a meaning. Thus, Kitcher appears to be correct in stating that, with religion – in this case, Perfect Being Theism – 'the reversals of this life will be compensated in the next'. Simply recognising this might offer the hope and comfort needed in the face of suffering. Due to its lack of detailed attributes, Pure Somethingism avoids the standard theoretical problem of evil but simultaneously (again due to the lack of details) fails to offer the kind of existential benefit that Perfect Being Theism does.

An objector might protest and suggest that Pure Strong Somethingism, because of its soteriological transcendency, actually implies an afterlife where suffering can be compensated. Schellenberg (2009: 32) has made this suggestion for soteriological ultimacy, but it seems impossible to generalise this conclusion to all soteriological transcendency. There are possible views of soteriological transcendency without an afterlife (like a heightened state of consciousness *in this life* only achievable through supernatural means). So there is no straightforward entailment between triple transcendence and an afterlife for victims of suffering. Perfect Being Theism, on the other hand, guarantees such compensation. Additionally, when endorsing a specific theistic view, like a Christian worldview, one accepts even more comforting details about, for example, heaven or a God who identifies with human suffering by becoming incarnate in Jesus Christ. Such details provide possibilities for both hope and consolation in a way that you just cannot find in Pure Strong Somethingism.

Naturally, one wonders if qualified versions of Somethingism can do better with respect to the existential challenge. In Old Religion Somethingism and New Spirituality Somethingism the thinning process often leaves many important details in place. However, qualified versions of Somethingism might encounter their own problems of evil, or at least embryos to such problems. Consider a None who reports to believe in 'something like a higher justice' or a 'good force on the side of life'. One might naturally ask how one can believe in the existence of a higher justice, if one is aware of the seemingly gratuitous suffering in the world? The argument is not conclusive like the one against Perfect Being Theism, but it challenges the None to explain what limits the higher justice or prevents the good force from abolishing suffering.

Another problem concerning suffering arises when we consider New Spirituality Somethingism of the nature-centred variety. These somethingists often report feelings of love of and connectedness with nature, in combination with deep existential or spiritual experiences of harmony and meaning. However, one might ask if these experiences reflect nature in any significant way. According to human standards, much interaction in nature is brutal and anything but harmonious. To see this point, just consider the inter-species interaction in the food chain, or how the evolutionary process and the survival of the fittest gives rise to an enormous amount of suffering in nature. Yujin Nagasawa (2018) has even described evolutionary suffering as a systemic evil. Acknowledging this, it is indeed very difficult to see nature as a place of hope and harmony.[43]

---

[43] In fact, the notion of nature as a place of harmony seems based on a Christian conception of nature as teleologically ordered by God.

Semi-Secular Worldviews and the Belief in Something Beyond   57

This is not meant to deny that detailed versions of Somethingism, including notions of greater goodness, a higher justice, or karmic principles, are superior to the pure versions when it comes to consolation, hope, and meaning. The 'thinning process' is not pursued to get rid of comforting ideas, but to discard aspects of traditional religions that are deemed pragmatically or epistemically inadequate. Any loss when it comes to existential resources must be regarded as collateral damage. It therefore seems safe to say that whether a version of Qualified Somethingism has the resources to cope with existential issues greatly depends on the specific details the view contains. Consider, for example, Paula from a study on privately religious people in Sweden. Paula expresses her thoughts on life after death not only by appealing to 'something', but also by talking about hope rather than belief. She states:

> I hope that there is something, but I don't know where and what. A lot of souls flying around, that doesn't work either. It's this again, that I don't want to mix God with the physical world. If there is to be any life after death, it is also on that side not ours. (Löwendahl 2005: 43)

This is clearly a kind of Life Question Somethingism, concerned with the afterlife. However, not many details remain in her exceptionally thin view, and, unfortunately for her, it seems that the kind of broad details she turns against are those with the potential to help when confronted with death or gratuitous suffering. By contrast, a more robust (say Christian) worldview comes with more of what we might call eschatological details which more exactly present what happens after death, how suffering might be redeemed, and so on.

To conclude, it seems that details are decisive when addressing all three problems discussed in this section. Pure versions of Somethingism cannot accommodate the alignment problem, nor can they play a religion-like role in the life of the None. They lack concrete content for moral action, and they also fail to adequately support the None in dealing with existential issues like gratuitous suffering.

The more qualified a version of Somethingism a None adheres to, the better her chances of addressing these issues. However, it's not just that details matter; the details must be relevant to the issue at hand. As we have seen, many Nones mix and match worldview components to create their own personalised worldviews, so whether they will end up having the most beneficial details or not in their views will vary greatly between individuals.

5 Summary and Future Research on Somethingism

Most Nones are not completely secularised; instead, they hold worldviews situated in the conceptual space between traditional religion and naturalism. With an emphasis on individuality and the epistemic authority of subjective well-being, these semi-secular Nones display an immense variety of worldviews, mixing and re-mixing from both traditional and new sources. While it seems impossible to identify a common denominator in the strict sense (we have been unable to find any non-trivial 'necessary condition' for having a semi-secular worldview), the closest we can get is that the ontological component of the worldviews of the Nones often contains general, unarticulated, and sometimes vague views about 'something' transcendent or at least transmundane. In line with the terminology already established by sociological scholars of religion, we refer to this view as Somethingism.

In Section 2, we developed Somethingism from individual remarks in sociological surveys into a full-fledged account worthy of philosophical attention, by using rational reconstruction and by introducing a new terminology. We have characterised Somethingism as the view that a Truly Significant Being (TSB) exists, which is immensely important, possibly life-enhancing, and a suitable object for serious commitment. Importantly, we distinguished between Strong Somethingism, according to which TSB is transcendent, and Weak Somethingism, according to which TSB is 'only' transmundane. We argued the TSB of the strong version must be metaphysically, soteriologically, and axiologically transcendent, thereby identifying it with Schellenberg's 'triply transcendent'.

Most Nones are not satisfied with the bare minimum provided by these most general views; they prefer versions of Somethingism with some level of detail. We therefore introduced the distinction between Pure and Qualified Somethingism, where the first is completely general while the latter contains some details about TSB. Finally, we distinguished between three kinds of Qualified Somethingism: Old Religion Somethingism (in which Somethingism is an abstraction of traditional religion), New Spirituality Somethingism (a spiritual commitment to a TSB), and Life Question Somethingism (Somethingism as an answer to certain life questions). We also identified three ways of thinning the content to reach Somethingism: thinning due to unacceptability, thinning due to insufficiency of language, and thinning due to ignorance.

In Section 3, we assessed Somethingism in relation to the epistemic challenge to worldviews. First, we considered the process of thinning itself, highlighting the important difference between generality (which is epistemically advantageous) and vagueness (which is philosophically problematic). While it is unquestionable that a general view always has a greater probability of being true than a detailed view on the same subject, it also seems that thinning all the way to Pure Somethingism represents an extreme epistemic position. As James and Levi remind us, avoiding falsehoods is not the only epistemic aim. We also want to believe true information. In this regard, Qualified Somethingism seems a more balanced trade-off between these aims.

Secondly, we considered Somethingism in relation to natural theology. Arguments in natural theology standardly consider how some phenomenon, like the fine-tuning of the universe or the existence of evil, can be explained by Perfect Being Theism and Naturalism. From the fact that the power of an explanation depends on the details of the explanatory theory, we concluded that it is doubtful whether Pure Weak Somethingism can explain anything. As it is a more substantial view, the prospects look better for Pure Strong Somethingism, but it is undeniable that Qualified Somethingism once again seems the better option. The best option, in our opinion, is Live Question Somethingism of a possible variety we do not find among the Nones, where the life question is identical with the questions posed by the different arguments in natural theology – like 'why does the universe seem fine-tuned for life?'.

Thirdly, we discussed the relation between Somethingism and non-doxasticism. We concluded that they represent different strategies to cope with unbelievable claims: thinning of attitude (non-doxasticism) and thinning of content (Somethingism). While we identified some instances where one strategy seems more suitable than the other, and some where a combination seem warranted, we did not find any reason to conclude that one strategy is superior to the other. However, we want to stress that this conclusion is preliminary, and that a more thorough investigation is needed to reach a definite conclusion.

We have only scratched the surface when it comes to the epistemological issues raised by Somethingism and the worldview of the Nones. One particularly interesting line of investigation outside the scope of this Element concerns the epistemological component of the Nones' worldview. As we have made clear, Nones are fierce epistemological individualists, who regard subjective experience as authoritative and their own personal well-being as a guide to truth. On the surface, and from a traditional epistemological perspective, this seems like a blatant conflation of epistemic and pragmatic reasons for belief. Is there any way of making sense of this epistemic stance without ascribing epistemic irrationality to the Nones?

Furthermore, there seems to be an inherent conflict between the Nones' self-reliant epistemology and the spread of semi-secular views, as understood from a social epistemological point of view. In short, semi-secular views seem to spread just like any other beliefs, by testimony through networks of epistemic agents. Many Nones also seem to have their own epistemic authorities, like wellness gurus, twelve-step instructors, and authors of self-help literature. Is there any way to make sense of this without rejecting the Nones' claims of epistemic self-reliance?

In Section 4, we examined whether Somethingism, in its various forms, could fulfill the role of traditional religion. We considered how somethingists can address the existential feasibility challenge. We began by discussing the alignment problem, which concerns the Nones' ability to interact with their TSB. We found this a relevant problem because Somethingism often lacks specific details, while we generally need to know at least some details of reality to effectively interact with it. We continued by considering more practical problems concerning whether or not somethingists can live a rich religious-like life – where, for example, moral action is a vital part – in a similar way as say a Christian can. Here, we reached the somewhat surprising conclusion that Pure Strong Somethingism must be a rare view in actuality, and we once again saw the benefits of Qualified Somethingism. We also reflected on the issue of whether Somethingism includes enough resources to cope with seemingly gratuitous suffering. We concluded that details do matter and that most general versions of Somethingism have a difficult time with these existential challenges and that Old Religion Somethingism, New Spirituality Somethingism, and Life Question Somethingism did better. However, not any content will be sufficient, but the details also need to be relevant for the issues at hand.

Of course, there are further existential challenges that Somethingism faces. One way to construct such challenges would be to follow Kitcher's procedure by considering the practical or existential benefits that conventional religion might offer, and ask whether Somethingism can provide the same benefits. Some examples that might be considered is whether or not something can incorporate a sense of final justice, or a purpose in life in the same sense as traditional religion. One further challenge that might be particularly troubling for Pure Somethingism is whether the worldview has the necessary resources to build a community, providing a sense of belonging. Kitcher argues that institutions connect their members by offering a sense of belonging together as well as a place to pursue common goals and talk about central issues in life (Kitcher 2011: 35). The communal life is not experienced in the same way in the West. In America, specifically, Kitcher notes that opportunities for fellowship, sympathetic relationships, the exchange of meaningful views, and the pursuit of important goals are not as prevalent outside churches and synagogues. In a secular setting, he writes, goals are formed and pursued alone (Kitcher 2011: 36–37).

There are several intriguing questions regarding the challenge of living a communal life and the benefits it entails. While it is true that the Nones are often individualists, they also seek out like-minded individuals on the internet and through political organisations. Can such activities compensate for the lack of communal life traditionally found in the Church? However, somethingists might face their own unique problem concerning this particular existential challenge. To live a fulfilling communal life, individuals need to share similar beliefs and strive for common goals. Do somethingists have the necessary content, or does the lack of details hinder the formation of a cohesive community? What kinds of goals are essential for such a communal life? These and other questions are key to consider in a world where the number of Nones is rapidly growing.

References

af Burén, Ann (2015) *Living Simultaneity*. Stockholm: Erlanders.

Alston, William (1996) 'Belief, Acceptance and Religious Faith'. Pages 3–27 in Jeff Jordan & Daniel Howard-Snyder (eds.), *Faith, Freedom, and Rationality*. London: Rowman and Littlefield Publishers Inc.

Berglund, Bruce (2018) *Castle and Cathedral in Modern Prague: Longing for the Sacred in a Skeptical Age*. Budapest: Central European University Press.

Bostrom, Nick (2003) 'Are We Living in a Computer Simulation?' *The Philosophical Quarterly* 53(211): 243–255.

Bramadat, Paul (2022) 'Reverential Naturalism in Cascadia: From the Fancy to the Sublime'. Pages 23–40 in Paul Bramadat, Patricia O'Connell Killen, & Sarah Wilkins-Laflamme (eds.), *Religion at the Edge: Nature, Spirituality and Secularity in the Pacific Northeast*. Vancouver: UBC Press.

Bråten, Oddrun (2022) 'Non-Binary Worldviews in Education'. *British Journal of Religious Education* 44(3): 325–333.

Burton, Tara (2020) *Strange Rites: New Religions for a Godless World*. New York: Public Affairs.

Chaves, Mark (2010) 'SSSR Presidential Address Rain Dances in the Dry Season: Overcoming the Religious Congruence Fallacy'. *Journal for the Scientific Study of Religion* 49(1): 1–14.

Collins, Robin (2009) 'The Teleological Argument: An Exploration of the Fine-Tuning of the Universe'. Pages 202–281 in William Lane Craig & James P. Moreland (eds.), *The Blackwell Companion to Natural Theology*. Oxford: Blackwell-Wiley.

Cottingham, John (2014) *Philosophy of Religion*. Cambridge: Cambridge University Press.

Couwenberg, Servatius W. (2005) 'Ietsisme is geloof van alle tijden'. *Trouw*, 18 January.

Davie, Grace (1994) *Religion in Britain since 1945: Believing without Belonging*. Oxford: Blackwell.

Demerath, Jay (2000) 'The Rise of "Cultural Religion" in European Christianity: Learning from Poland, Northern Ireland, and Sweden'. *Social Compass* 47(1): 127–139.

Dole, Andrew (2013) 'Is Sceptical Religion Adequate as a Religion?' *Religious Studies* 49(2): 235–248.

Elliott, James (2017) 'The Power of Humility in Sceptical Religion: Why Ietsism Is Preferable to J. L. Schellenberg's Ultimism'. *Religious Studies* 53(1): 97–116.

Fine, Kit (2020) *Vagueness: A Global Approach*. Oxford: Oxford University Press.

Gan, Peter (2022) 'Is There Something Worthwhile in Somethingism?' *European Journal for Philosophy of Religion* 14(4): 171–193.

Greene, Brian (2011) *The Hidden Reality: Parallel Universes and the Deep Laws of the Cosmos*. New York: Vintage.

Heelas, Paul, & Woodhead, Linda (2005) *The Spiritual Revolution: Why Religion Is Giving Way to Spirituality*. Malden: Blackwell Publishing.

Holstein, E. J. N. (2020) *Een zinvol leven: een filosofisch perspectief*. Barendrecht: Reflectera.

Howard-Snyder, Daniel (2013) 'Propositional Faith: What It Is and What It Is Not'. *American Philosophical Quarterly* 50(4): 357–372.

James, William (2010 (1897)) *The Will to Believe and Other Essays in Popular Philosophy, and Human Immortality*. Milton Keynes: Digireads.com Publishing.

Jenkins, Jack (2019) '"Nones" Now as Big as Evangelicals, Catholics in the US'. Religion News Service, 21 March, https://religionnews.com/2019/03/21/nones-now-as-big-as-evangelicals-catholics-in-the-us/.

Jonbäck, Francis (2022) 'Hopeism'. *Studia Theologica – Nordic Journal of Theology* 76(2):172–192.

Jonbäck, Francis, & Palmqvist, Carl-Johan (2024) 'Between Belief and Disbelief, between Religion and Secularity: Introducing Non-Doxasticism and Semi-Secularity in Worldview Education'. *British Journal of Religious Education* 46(2): 109–121.

Kahane, Guy (2011) 'Should We Want God to Exist?'.' *Philosophy and Phenomenological Research* 82(3): 674–696.

Kitcher, Philip (2011) 'Challenges for Secularism'. Pages 24–56 in George Levine (ed.), *The Joy of Secularism*. Princeton: Princeton University Press.

Leech, David (2020) '"New Agnosticism", Imaginative Challenge, and Religious Experience'. Pages 107–139 in Francis Fallon & Gavin Hyman (eds.), *Agnosticism: Explorations in Philosophy and Religious Thought*. Oxford: Oxford University Press.

Lemos, Carlos, & Puga-Gonzalez, Ivan (2021) 'Belief in God, Confidence in the Church and Secularization in Scandinavia'. *Secularism and Nonreligion* 10(5): 1–21.

Levi, Isaac (1967) *Gambling with Truth: An Essay on Induction and the Aims of Science*. Cambridge, MA: MIT Press.

Linville, Mark D. (2009) 'The Moral Argument'. Pages 391–448 in William Lane Craig & James P. Moreland (eds.), *The Blackwell Companion to Natural Theology*. Oxford: Blackwell-Wiley.

Löwendahl, L. (2005). *Religion utan organisation: om religiös rörlighet bland privatreligiösa*. Östlings bokförlag Symposion.

Lougheed, Kirk (2020) *The Axiological Status of Theism and Other Worldviews*. Cham: Palgrave Macmillan.

Manson, Neil A. 2003 'Introduction' in Neil A. Manson (ed.) *God and Design* (1–23) London: Routledge.

Mercadante, Linda A. (2014) *Belief without Borders: Inside the Minds of the Spiritual but not Religious*. Oxford: Oxford University Press.

Mercadante, Linda A. (2020) 'Spiritual Struggles of Nones and "Spiritual But Not Religious" (SBNRs)'. *Religions* 11 (10): 513.

Nagasawa, Yujin (2018) 'The Problem of Evil for Atheists'. Pages 151–163 in Nick Trakakis (ed.), *The Problem of Evil – Eight Views in Dialogue*. Oxford: Oxford University Press.

Nagel, Thomas (2010) *Secular Philosophy and the Religious Temperament*. Oxford: Oxford University Press.

Norris, Pippa, & Inglehart, Ronald (2011) *Sacred and Secular: Religion and Politics Worldwide*. 2nd ed. New York: Cambridge University Press.

Oppy, Graham (2006) *Arguing about Gods*. Cambridge: Cambridge University Press.

Oppy, Graham (2013) *The Best Argument against God*. Cham: Palgrave Macmillan.

Palmqvist, Carl-Johan (2019) 'The Proper Object of Non-Doxastic Religion: Why Traditional Religion Should Be Preferred Over Schellenberg's Ultimism'. *Religious Studies* 55(4): 559–574.

Palmqvist, Carl-Johan (2021) 'Forms of Belief-Less Religion: Why Non-Doxasticism Makes Fictionalism Redundant for the Pro-Religious Agnostic'. *Religious Studies* 57(1): 49–65.

Palmqvist, Carl-Johan (2022) 'A Faith for the Future'. *European Journal for Philosophy of Religion* 14(1): 95–122.

Palmqvist, Carl-Johan (2023) 'The Old Gods as a Live Possibility: On the Rational Feasibility of Non-Doxastic Paganism'. *Religious Studies* 59(4): 651–664.

Palmqvist, Carl-Johan, & Jonbäck, Francis (2023) 'On the Rationality of Semi-Secular Simultaneity: A Non-Doxastic Interpretation of the Seemingly

Inconsistent Worldviews of Some Swedish "Nones"'. *Religious Studies* 59(4): 589–602.

Pearce, Kenneth L. (2017) 'Foundational Grounding and the Argument from Contingency'. In Jonathan L. Kvanvig (ed.), *Oxford Studies in Philosophy of Religion* 8: 245–268. Oxford: Oxford University Press.

Penner, Myron (2015) 'Personal Anti-Theism and the Meaningful Life Argument'. *Faith and Philosophy* 32(3): 325–337.

Pew Research Center (2009) 'Many Americans Mix Multiple Faiths'. 9 December. www.pewresearch.org/religion/2009/12/09/many-americans-mix-multiple-faiths/.

Pew Research Center (2013) 'Canada's Changing Religious Landscape'. 27 June. www.pewresearch.org/religion/2013/06/27/canadas-changing-religious-landscape/.

Pew Research Center (2024) 'Religious "Nones" in America: Who They Are and What They Believe'. 24 January. www.pewresearch.org/religion/2024/01/24/religious-nones-in-america-who-they-are-and-what-they-believe/#q2-why-are-nones-nonreligious.

Plantinga, Alvin (2011) *Where the Conflict Really Lies: Science, Religion and Naturalism*. Oxford: Oxford University Press.

Pojman, Louis (1986) 'Faith without Belief'. *Faith and Philosophy* 3(2): 157–176.

Pruss, Alexander R. (2009) 'The Liebnizian Cosmological Argument'. Pages 24–100 in William L. Craig & James P. Moreland (eds.), *The Blackwell Companion to Natural Theology*. Oxford: Blackwell-Wiley.

Rowe, William (2006) 'Friendly Atheism, Skeptical Theism and the Problem of Evil'. *International Journal for Philosophy of Religion* 59(2): 79–92.

Schellenberg, John L. (2005) *Prolegomena to a Philosophy of Religion*. Ithaca, NY: Cornell University Press.

Schellenberg, John L. (2009) *The Will to Imagine*. Ithaca, NY: Cornell University Press.

Schellenberg, John L. (2013) *Evolutionary Religion*. Oxford: Oxford University Press.

Schellenberg, John L. (2019a) *Progressive Atheism*. London: Bloomsbury Academic.

Schellenberg, John L. (2019b) *Religion after Science*. Cambridge: Cambridge University Press.

Siniscalchi, Glenn B. (2018) 'Contemporary Trends in Atheistic Criticism of Thomistic Natural Theology.' *Heythrop Journal* 59(4): 689–706.

Sober, Elliott (2003). 'The Design Argument' in Neil A. Manson (ed.) *God and Design* (25–53) London: Routledge.

Sober, Elliott (2019) *The Design Argument*. Cambridge: Cambridge University Press.

Sorenson, Roy (2022) 'Vagueness'. *Stanford Encyclopedia of Philosophy*, accessed 1 December 2023, https://plato.stanford.edu/entries/vagueness/.

Steinhart, Eric C. (2014) *Your Digital Afterlives: Computational Theories of Life and Death* London: Palgrave Macmillan.

Stenmark, Mikael (1995) *Rationality in Science, Religion and Everyday Life*. Notre Dame, IN: University of Notre Dame Press.

Stenmark, Mikael (2022a) 'Secular Worldviews: Scientific Naturalism and Secular Humanism' *European Journal for Philosophy of Religion* 12(4):237–264.

Stenmark, Mikael (2022b) 'Worldview Studies'. *Religious Studies* 58(3):564–582.

Swinburne, Richard (2004 (1979)) *The Existence of God*. 2nd ed. Oxford: Oxford University Press.

Taliaferro, Charles (2009) 'The Project of Natural Theology'.' Pages 1–23 in William L. Craig & James P. Moreland (eds.), *The Blackwell Companion to Natural Theology*. Oxford: Blackwell-Wiley.

Taves, Ann (2020) 'From Religious Studies to Worldview Studies'. *Religion* 50(1):137–147.

Taylor, Charles (1989) *Sources of the Self*. Cambridge, MA: Harvard University Press.

Taylor, Charles (1991) *The Ethics of Authenticity*. Cambridge, MA: Harvard University Press.

Taylor, Charles (2002) 'Modern Social Imaginaries'. *Public Culture* 14(1): 91–124.

Taylor, Charles (2007) *A Secular Age*. Cambridge, MA: Harvard University Press.

Thurfjell, David (2015) *Det gudlösa folket. De postkristna svenskarna och religionen*. Stockholm: Molin & Sorgenfrei.

Thurfjell, David (2020) *Granskogsfolket*. Stockholm: Norstedts.

Thurfjell, David, Rubow, Cecilie, Remmel, Atko, & Ohlsson, Henrik (2019) 'The Relocation of Transcendence: Using Schutz to Conceptualize the Nature Experiences of Secular People'. *Nature and Culture* 14(2): 190–214.

Voas, David (2009) 'The Rise and Fall of Fuzzy Fidelity in Europe'. *European Sociological Review* 25(2): 155–168.

Wilkins-Laflamme, Sarah (2014). 'Towards Religious Polarization? Time Effects on Religious Commitment in US, UK and Canadian Regions'. *Sociology of Religion* 75(2):284–308.

Wilkins-Laflamme, Sarah (2022) 'Second to None: Nonaffiliation in the Pacific Northwest'. Page 100 in Paul Bramadat, Patricia Oconnell Killen, & Sarah Wilkins-Laflamme (eds.), *Religion on the Edge*. Toronto: UBC Press.

Willander, Erika (2015), 'Religiositet och sekularisering'. Pages 53–68 in *Sociologiska perspektiv på religion i Sverige*. Falkenberg: Gleerups.

Willander, Erika (2020) *Unity, Division and the Religious Mainstream of Sweden*. Cham: Palgrave.

Zuckerman, Phill (2009) 'Why Are Danes and Swedes so Irreligious?'. *Nordic Journal of Religion and Society* 22(1): 55–69.

Acknowledgements

Research for the book was funded by Åke Wibergs Foundation [Project: "Beyond Faith"]; and the Swedish Science Council [Project: 2018–01050].

Cambridge Elements ≡

Global Philosophy of Religion

Yujin Nagasawa
University of Oklahoma
Yujin Nagasawa is Kingfisher College Chair of the Philosophy of Religion and Ethics and Professor of Philosophy at the University of Oklahoma. He is the author of *The Problem of Evil for Atheists* (2024), *Maximal God: A New Defence of Perfect Being Theism* (2018), *Miracles: A Very Short Introduction* (2018), *The Existence of God: A Philosophical Introduction* (2011), and *God and Phenomenal Consciousness* (2008), along with numerous articles. He is the editor-in-chief of *Religious Studies* and served as the president of the British Society for the Philosophy of Religion from 2017 to 2019.

About the Series
This Cambridge Elements series provides concise and structured overviews of a wide range of religious beliefs and practices, with an emphasis on global, multi-faith viewpoints. Leading scholars from diverse cultural backgrounds and geographical regions explore topics and issues that have been overlooked by Western philosophy of religion.

Cambridge Elements⁼

Global Philosophy of Religion

Elements in the Series

Afro-Brazilian Religions
José Eduardo Porcher

The African Mood Perspective on God and the Problem of Evil
Ada Agada

Contemporary Pagan Philosophy
Eric Steinhart

Semi-Secular Worldviews and the Belief in Something Beyond
Carl-Johan Palmqvist and Francis Jonbäck

A full series listing is available at: www.cambridge.org/EGPR

For EU product safety concerns, contact us at Calle de José Abascal, 56–1°, 28003 Madrid, Spain or eugpsr@cambridge.org.

www.ingramcontent.com/pod-product-compliance
Lightning Source LLC
LaVergne TN
LVHW020352260326
834688LV00045B/1673